MW01242694

Change, Lead & Grow

The 5 Proven Steps to Achieve Ongoing Success

María de Lourdes González, MBA, PE, PMP

Special **<u>FREE</u>** Bonus Gift for You!

To help you achieve more success, there are **FREE BONUS RESOURCES FOR YOU** at:

www.FreeGiftFromMLG.com

informational purposes only. Use caution and see the advice of qualified professionals. Check with your accountant, attorney or professional advisor before acting on this or any information. You agree that María de Lourdes González and/or ML Growth Consulting Group, Inc. is not responsible for the success or failure of your personal, business, health or financial decisions relating to any information presented by María de Lourdes González, ML Growth Consulting Group, Inc., or company products/services. Earnings potential is entirely dependent on the efforts, skills and application of the individual person. Any examples, stories, references, or case studies are for illustrative purposes only and should not be interpreted as testimonies and/or examples of what reader and/or consumers can generally expect from the information. No representation in any part of this information, materials and/or seminar training are guarantees or promises for actual performance. Any statements, strategies, concepts, techniques, exercises and ideas in the information, materials and/or seminar training offered are simply opinion or experience, and thus should not be misinterpreted as promises, typical results or guarantees (expressed or implied). The author and publisher (María de Lourdes González, ML Growth Consulting Group, Inc. (MLG) or any of MLG's representatives) shall in no way, under any circumstances, be held liable to any party (or third party) for any direct, indirect, punitive, special, incidental or other consequential damages arising directly or indirectly from any use of books, materials and or seminar trainings, which is provided "as is," and without warranties.

What Others Are Saying About María de Lourdes González

"I've known Lourdes for many years. She has been a great asset to the team, adding value and providing effective change management solutions using a pragmatic collaborative approach. Her cross-functional perspectives and experience make complex scopes easier to handle under a clear change management framework."

— **Luis Mustafa**
VP Innovation & Operational Excellence

"Throughout my extensive experience in the pharmaceutical industry, I have witnessed María de Lourdes' ability to guide people in identifying areas that require improvement. Her expertise in facilitating change is truly commendable. She has a genuine commitment to ensure that we apply what we've learned to achieve our goals."

— **Jennifer Biaggi**
Chief Pharmacist - Universal Care Corporation

"Lourdes is a true catalyst for change. She has a solid track record of identifying areas of improvement and developing actionable strategies that deliver measurable results."

— **Kevin Cook**
VP Global Pharmaceuticals Supply Chain

"Lourdes' exceptional skills in defining technical concepts and processes easily understood makes her an invaluable asset for any organization who wishes to grow and succeed."

— **Andrés Vázquez**
Supply Chain Executive

"This book is the secret weapon and blueprint that every person, leader or professional can use to achieve success in their business, their career, and in life. María de Lourdes González has put together a unique collection of life's lessons and personal success strategies to overcome change, lead others, and grow. Her book is incredibly noteworthy, valuable and inspiring to help you build confidence and reach your goals to achieve success. Change, Lead & Grow is truly magical! Well done!"

— **John Formica**
The "Ex-Disney Guy", America's Best Customer Experience Speaker and Coach

"María de Lourdes' expertise empowers individuals to embrace change as a catalyst for professional and personal growth, unlocking hidden potential. This is a must-read book!"

— **Jill Lublin**
4x Best Selling Author, International Speaker,
Master Publicity Strategist

"Having worked with Lourdes as my mentor for many years, I have witnessed her leadership skills and change mindset and for sure will get you where you want to be. She always fosters collaboration at different levels and functions to assure adoption of initiatives from executives to end users."

— **Amaury Maldonado, PMP**
Continuous Improvement Consultant

"María de Lourdes' strategies have the power to embrace change as an opportunity for growth."

— **Megan Unsworth**
Cofounder of LifeOnFire.com,
Queen of Coaching

Motivate and Inspire Others!

Special Quantity Discounts

5-20 Books	$17.95
21-99 Books	$16.95
100-499 Books	$14.95
500-999 Books	Inquire

Special Discount Pricing is subject to change.
Please contact us for final pricing options.

To Place an Order Contact:

Info@MLGrowth.com

The Ideal Professional Speaker for Your Next Event!

Any organization that wants to develop their people to become "extraordinary," needs to hire María de Lourdes González for a keynote and/or workshop training!

To Contact or Book María de Lourdes González to Speak:

Info@MLGrowth.com

The Ideal Consultant and Coach for You!

If you're ready to overcome challenges, have major break-throughs and achieve higher levels, then you will love having María de Lourdes González as your consultant and coach!

To Contact María de Lourdes González:

Lourdes.Gonzalez@MLGrowth.com

Dedication

With profound gratitude and boundless love, I dedicate this book to my parents, family, and friends. Your unwavering support and encouragement have been the guiding light in all my endeavors. Thank you for being by my side throughout this beautiful journey!

I love you all!

To all those who believe in the transformative power of change and strive to make a positive difference in the world, this dedication is for you. May our collective efforts shape a brighter future for generations to come.

Table of Contents

A Message to You!

It all began with a change. The world stopped. Everything changed… But this time was different. We all had to adapt. The importance of effectively managing changes became more evident in our lives, and it was no easy task. Many areas require consideration, with some being easier than others. I've seen this every day, given that I've dedicated my entire career to helping people implement changes within their businesses.

During these unprecedented times, I witnessed many people struggling and without the right tools to navigate change successfully. These experiences have enlightened me, showing that my journey could inspire and empower others to take action. I never thought about writing a book before, but as I observed the challenges and gaps people were facing, I realized there was a need for guidance. This book is the result of that realization - a guide crafted to equip you and your team with the tools needed to embrace and drive change effectively within your organization.

Life is full of changes, and learning how to navigate them is essential. Sometimes change can be scary, and oftentimes, it is complicated. But through it all, change is the catalyst for growth. I can assure you that embracing change will lead you to new heights.

As a professional, I've spent years implementing changes, improving processes, managing projects, and achieving results while considering the crucial elements of people, processes, and technology. Each change allowed me to learn and implement tools that streamlined the process. I wish I had a useful resource like this book earlier in my career— it would have made navigating changes faster and easier. That's why I want to share this knowledge with you wherever you are in your business journey. I hope that this book will be a valuable companion for you.

Many years ago, I was hired by a company to lead the implementation of a manufacturing execution system from its beginning phases – selecting the team to work with the changes – up to delivering the new solution to the business. The objective was to reduce errors, cycle time, and inventory, improve product yield, and increase productivity while providing additional capacity for more production and growing the business. The change was transitioning from a paper batch record of 300 pages to an electronic batch record.

Sounds simple, right? Far from it. It was more than that.

This implementation had multiple dimensions related to people, processes, and systems. Along the way, I had the opportunity to use the tools and strategies that I will share with you in this book...

We are all in this together. Change is constant, happening everywhere, and businesses face endless changes. These can range from new regulations, marketplace challenges, and evolving customer and supplier dynamics to technological advancements, environmental shifts, process improvements, and new ways of working.

Change is not a straightforward process—it can impact multiple areas of your organization. To ensure effective and lasting changes, you need to consider all the areas. Whether your change is a small adjustment or a large-scale transformation, the steps outlined here are tailored to your needs. Simpler changes may require simpler steps, while more complex changes demand comprehensive solutions. It's important to recognize that change ideas can come from anyone in the organization. Engaging everyone is vital for fresh perspectives. The success of these changes relies on teamwork and support, not just individual actions.

In this book, you will discover a valuable tool that can empower you and your team to navigate change with confidence and achieve remarkable results in your business. By applying the principles and strategies outlined in these chapters, you will unlock a world of possibilities and position yourself for ongoing success.

You'll find the solution that integrates various tools to help you implement lasting changes and achieve tangible results in your business. This framework complements your project management methodology, integrating concepts from managing changes, business processes and projects. It applies to various areas including strategic planning, people development, system implementations, supply chain improvements, and more.

Integrated Methodology Elements

Change

Assess business needs and implement changes to manage and sustain new ways of working

Business Process

Assess and deliver business process solutions from definition to implementation

Project

Align with project methodology to deliver solutions to achieve organization goals

Imagine having the ability to steer your organization through any change, big or small, and emerge stronger, more resilient, and more competitive than ever before. This book will equip you with the knowledge, insights, and practical tools necessary to make that vision a reality.

Now, I invite you to use this framework to evaluate opportunities and effectively implement the changes you desire. Select a current project or initiative in your business that could benefit from a fresh approach. How can you incorporate this to drive impactful change and achieve tangible results? Reflect on a recent change initiative in your organization that faced obstacles or fell short of expectations. How can the concepts and strategies outlined here make a difference? What specific actions could you have taken to overcome those challenges?

Take a moment to envision the future of your business. What do you aspire to achieve? How can the principles from this book guide you and your team in shaping that future and navigating the necessary changes to get there?

The need for ongoing success and growth in business is undeniable. By implementing the steps outlined in this book, you will consistently achieve results and stay ahead of the competition. Being open to new ideas and innovative approaches empowers you to remain relevant, competitive, and profitable in today's dynamic marketplace. Embracing change opens doors to new possibilities, fosters innovation, and enhances operational efficiency.

Share this book with your team members, colleagues, friends, and family, and together, let's make positive changes in the world!

It is an honor to connect with you through this book. I hope we have the opportunity to meet in person soon. Wishing you tremendous growth and success on your journey!

María de Lourdes González

Are you ready?

"Embrace change, be the catalyst of transformation, and shape the future with your actions."

Change is Constant...

"Change is the source of improvement and innovation."

In business, you face constant streams of changes in various areas. Consider the changes you're presently handling. With multiple projects happening simultaneously, you may be looking for opportunities to navigate through these changes more effectively.

Like many companies and organizations, you may encounter challenges in achieving your goals and aligning the available tools and methodologies due to competing priorities, resource constraints, and financial limitations among others. Additionally, specific resistance to change can manifest as fear and reluctance among those directly involved or potentially affected, such as end-users or customers. You need to address this resistance and ensure that your team is entirely on board, invested, and equipped to manage any changes that come your way. Embracing change is the key to long-term success.

To remain competitive and relevant, you need to be both agile and adaptable while providing exceptional value to your clients and customers. This requires skillfully navigating a constantly changing landscape, which includes overcoming obstacles such as shifting customer expectations, learning from innovative competitors, and keeping up with emerging technological advancements.

A Comprehensive Approach for Ongoing Success

Tailored specifically for business leaders, project managers, entrepreneurs, solopreneurs, and those committed to consistent growth, this book offers a comprehensive methodology. It integrates key elements from business process management, project management, and change management. This integrated approach sets the stage for effectively managing changes that drive continuous growth and success.

The Five Steps of Achieving Success

Successful change implementation can be integrated and applied using the five steps on page 9.

This framework offers practical guidance to integrate changes across people, processes, systems, and resources. By integrating these steps, your organization can address challenges and unlock new opportunities for success, leading to:

- **Enhanced efficiency and productivity** through strategic changes, streamlined processes, and optimized resource utilization.

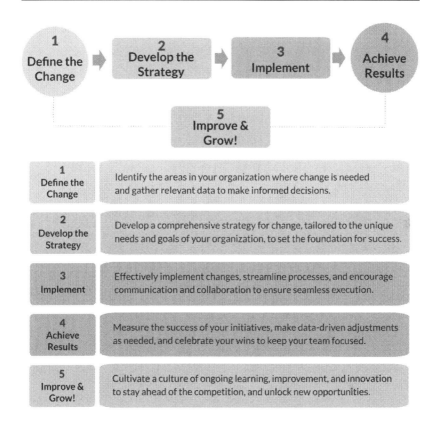

- **Improved communication and collaboration** among team members, leading to successful change initiatives.

- **Enhanced adaptability and agility,** allowing rapid responses to evolving market trends, customer needs, and technological advance

- **Improved employee satisfaction and engagement**, as effective change implementation empowers team members to contribute meaningfully.

- **Increased profitability and growth** achieved by identifying areas for enhancement, implementing effective strategies, and attaining measurable results.

To stay ahead of the competition and prepare your organization for long-term success, you need to be aware and responsive to emerging trends, developments, and innovations.

The Increasing Role of Technology

Embracing change means keeping up with innovations. In recent years, you may have experienced how fast technology has emerged as a significant driver of business transformation. With these advancements taking the lead, including **Artificial Intelligence (AI),** organizations are empowered to streamline processes, make data-driven decisions and unlock unprecedented breakthroughs, ultimately leading to increased profits and growth.

Although obstacles may arise on the path to transformation, technology can make lives easier and better. It is important to develop and unleash better systems and processes to manage rapid changes through technological advancements. Strong capabilities in managing change effectively are essential for organizations.

Your Growth Journey Begins

In this section, you have found how implementing change effectively leads to growth. Utilizing each of the five steps outlined in this book will offer you valuable insights on how to adapt to evolving market conditions and emerging work methodologies. This book will be your companion in formulating a transformational strategy, taking confident and determined steps, and ultimately achieving success.

Throughout this book, you will find various examples that provide practical insights into implementing the framework.

⇒ Examples will be referenced in bullets as shown here, for easier reference.

Additional Resources and Perspectives

In **Section II - Toolkit,** you will find templates that can be customized to suit the specific needs and characteristics of your organization and change initiative.

Visit **www.FreeGiftFromMLG.com** to find resources that complement this book. Explore our **eBook**, **'Change, Lead & Grow - Business Insights,'** which includes scenarios from a manufacturing company, a small business, and a solopreneur. These scenarios offer diverse perspectives and demonstrate the practical application of the framework's tools in different settings.

You can also access other valuable resources including areas of opportunity where technology, including AI, plays a key role in driving business growth. We hope that these tools will equip you with a holistic understanding necessary in today's dynamic business landscape.

Allow the five-step process outlined in this book to empower and guide you in driving change and fostering growth within your organization, enabling you to plan and achieve ongoing success.

To your success!

"The pursuit of excellence yields remarkable results."

Section I

The 5 Steps to Achieve Ongoing Success

Step 1
Define the Change

"Change is the gateway to greater opportunities."

Having the opportunity to implement changes throughout my career, which involves dealing with process improvements, enterprise systems implementations, and technology transfers, one of the most impactful was the implementation of electronic batch record.

Going Paperless: Electronic Batch Record Project

The manufacturing industry relies on batch records to track the production process and ensure compliance with regulations. Previously, batch records were created and maintained on paper. However, with advancements in technology, electronic batch records have become more common and needed.

The transition from paper to electronic batch records required changes to the production process and the implementation of new software, hardware, and equipment. Quality control and compliance are also important areas that are impacted by the transition from paper to electronic batch records... but the manufacturing employees were greatly impacted, since at that time, they had limited experience with electronic systems. (Remember this was many years ago!) It was a big change for them! It was necessary to provide training and support so they could learn new skills and adapt to new ways of working.

This change provided many benefits, but it also impacted different areas of the manufacturing process.

Some of the benefits identified were:

- real-time data

- improved accuracy and traceability

- easier access to information

- easily searchable

- can be accessed by multiple individuals at once

- can be easily backed up and store

- save time and resources

- improved efficiency

Additionally, electronic records are more secure and reduce the risk of errors, as they can be programmed to enforce certain rules and validations, resulting in better compliance with regulatory requirements.

To successfully implement the transition from paper to electronic batch records, the achievement of the desired outcomes became the priority. It required investing significant effort in identifying people, process and system areas where change was needed (from batch record creation, weigh dispensing, manufacturing execution and product release) and developing a comprehensive plan to achieve the goals. At the end of each step, you will find more information about this project.

Implementing change is not a one-person job. Effective leadership plays a crucial role in building a cohesive team with a shared vision and ensuring that all aspects of the change are properly addressed.

As a leader, you need to recognize the important role that people play in implementing change. By providing a clear vision, setting the tone, and allocating the necessary resources and support, you will inspire your people to engage in the change process and work towards a common goal. With the foundation of effective leadership and a well-defined plan, you can navigate the complexities of change and drive successful outcomes.

Let's begin by understanding the change!

Understanding the Change

In this step, you will learn how to define the change you are trying to make in a way that is clear, concise, and actionable, regardless on the business you are in.

A **manufacturing company** leader is determined to stream-line their supply chain and reduce costs. A **small business** owner is committed to implementing a cloud-based filing system to enhance efficiency, reduce costs and elevate the customer experience. A **solopreneur** is focused on adopting new marketing strategies to expand the business and increase earnings by attracting more clients.

What do they all have in common?

Aside from determination, commitment, and focus, they all want to improve their productivity and efficiency, to become more profitable. Ultimately, their goal is to achieve ongoing success and growth.

What is the Change?

Change is a critical component of any thriving business. Admittedly, it can also be challenging to execute. Many businesses struggle to implement change effectively, which can result in wasted resources, dissatisfied employees, and unsuccessful projects.

However, one way to look at making changes is that it presents an opportunity for growth and progress. While change may disrupt the status quo, it also opens possibilities for improvement and innovation. Additionally, investing in new resources such as equipment, software, or training can ultimately lead to greater efficiency and productivity. Finally, taking the time to implement changes carefully and thoughtfully can lead to a more successful outcome and can ultimately benefit the organization in the long run. Yes, there may be risks along the way, but there are also several things you can do to improve your chances of implementing change effectively.

One thing is to create a **clear and compelling vision for change**. What are your desired outcomes? What are your short-term and long-term goals? People need to understand these along with the purpose and goal of the change so they can involve themselves and own the process. They also are more likely to be supportive of the change if they feel like they have a say in it.

After articulating your vision and goals, you must consider how the change aligns with them. Doing so will help you understand the **impact of the change** along with the metrics or indicators you need to consider in measuring success. Do you aim for an increase in sales? Do you intend to reduce costs? Are you seeking to invest in employee productivity? Are you actively campaigning for greater customer satisfaction? Or would you like to focus on improving your brand reputation?

By reflecting on these questions and eventually answering them, you will gain vital insights on how to better align the change with your vision and goals.

This process will help you clarify your intentions, define the change, and understand your desired outcomes. It means identifying the specific problem or opportunity that is driving the change, understanding its root cause and planning the desired outcome. This process can also uncover potential challenges or obstacles that may arise during the change, allowing you to proactively address them and minimize any negative impacts.

Different areas are impacted by the types of change. You may allocate some time with key people to brainstorm and gather information on those areas and visualize the future state from many angles. For example, some business changes may involve:

- **Organization:** Restructuring departments or creating new ones.

- **Process:** Implementing new procedures or policies, altering the way things are done.

- **Behavioral:** Changing attitudes or habits, influencing the way people behave.

- **Technological:** Incorporating new tools and equipment, adopting new software or hardware

By thoughtfully considering these, the succeeding steps for defining the change will be much easier to navigate.

"Change presents an opportunity for growth and progress. Embrace it as a catalyst for improvement and innovation."

What are the Drivers of the Change?

The drivers of change are the factors or forces that initiate and motivate the change process.

These can be classified into two categories: internal and external. Internal drivers originate from within the organization itself, while external drivers stem from factors outside the organization's immediate control. It's important to differentiate between these two types of drivers to gain a comprehensive understanding of the forces that initiate and influence change.

External drivers of change may include:

- **Market and Industry Changes:** Fluctuations in market trends, emergence of new competitors, and changing consumer preferences

- **Customer Needs:** Consumer demands and expectations towards company offerings, services, or delivery methods

- **Compliance Requirements:** Legislation and guidelines related to data privacy laws, environmental regulations, and conformity to industry standards

- **Technological Advancements:** Development and rise of automation, robotics, artificial intelligence, social media, and communication technologies

- **Social and Political Factors:** Changes in government policies, cultural values, and public priorities, alongside social movements and international events

Internal drivers of change, on the other hand, may include:

- **Internal Inefficiencies:** Resisting change, lack of innovation, overcomplicated organization structure, inadequate resources, and poor communication

- **Outdated Technologies:** Utilizing obsolete software or hardware, security or privacy vulnerabilities, limiting capacity for innovation

- **Low Employee Morale:** Persisting negative work culture, inadequate employee development opportunities, micromanagement and demotivation

- **Employee Retention and Engagement:** Providing competitive compensation and benefits packages, career growth, and positive management practices

- **Organizational Growth and Development:** Scaling up operations, exploring new resources, training capabilities for new processes and workflows

- **New Opportunities:** Forming partnerships, entry into new markets, expansion of products or service offerings, introduction of new systems and technology

By understanding the drivers of change, organizations can evaluate the potential impact of these forces, identify opportunities for growth and improvement, and develop effective strategies for managing and adapting to change. This knowledge enables businesses to prioritize initiatives, allocate resources effectively, and communicate the purpose and necessity of the transformation to stakeholders.

Ultimately, recognizing and comprehending the drivers of change empowers organizations to navigate the dynamic business landscape, seize opportunities for growth, and drive meaningful and successful transformations.

Why is the Change Needed?

Having identified the drivers of change, it's time to define the underlying reasons and motivations behind the transformation. Why is this change happening? Is it driven by emerging market trends, evolving customer demands, technological advancements, competitive pressures, or the need for operational efficiency? By revealing the underlying motivations and benefits, you can effectively communicate a captivating vision that guides your team toward a future filled with success.

A compelling case for change should outline the reasons, benefits, and impact of the proposed changes. You need to articulate the reason behind it as clearly and as effectively as possible.

Some examples are:

⇒ **Manufacturing Facility:** To address bottlenecks and inefficiencies, improve operational efficiency, and enhance customer satisfaction through real-time visibility and accuracy in inventory management.

⇒ **Small Business:** To streamline processes, improve accuracy, optimize space utilization, and enhance the customer experience.

⇒ **Solopreneur:** To increase earnings and achieve business growth while continuing to deliver excellent customer service.

Based on experience, major changes are often triggered by a variety of factors, as previously enumerated. However, a good way to help you understand the "why" is by knowing your motivation and purpose.

You have to make sure that it is also relevant how you wish to impact your stakeholders, customers, employees, and partners.

Highlighting the significance of articulating the reasons for change empowers you to inspire and motivate your team on the exciting journey that lies ahead.

How does the Change align with the Vision?

Do you agree that businesses need to constantly revisit and reframe their vision and objectives? If yes, are you doing this consistently? When you make a change, you want to make sure that the change aligns with the vision and goals of the organization. This involves understanding how the change will impact your business, values, culture, and how it fits into your long-term strategy.

⇒ If the organization's vision is to become the market leader in their industry, a change that involves investing in new technology or expanding to new markets would align with that vision.

⇒ If your vision is to achieve operational excellence, you may decide to leverage technology to enhance efficiency, improve accuracy, and elevate the customer experience.

Another scenario is when a **small business** that values personal connections with its customers wants to implement technology-based customer service tools that maintain a personal touch. It certainly will need to integrate customer service tools that prioritize personalization and individualized attention.

"Aligning change with the strategic vision empowers progress, drives the business towards its desired destination, and ensures a unified journey with everyone on board."

All of these examples highlight the importance of aligning the change with the business's values and goals. By ensuring that the change is in line with the organization's vision, you can drive progress and foster a sense of purpose and direction throughout the organization.

Benefits and Risks

Identifying the potential benefits and risks of change helps you make informed decisions, effectively communicate their value to stakeholders, and increase buy-in and support. By doing so early in the process, you can maximize the positive impact of the change on both the business and its stakeholders. This will help you set the strategies for the changes, establish messages for engagement and create plans to mitigate risk.

In assessing the benefits and risks, ask yourself several key questions:

- **Improved Efficiency:** Will the change streamline business processes, save time, and maximize resources? Consider how the change can optimize workflow, eliminate bottlenecks and improve overall operational efficiency.

- **Improved Customer Experience:** Will the change result in higher customer satisfaction, increased brand awareness, and loyalty? Explore how the change can enhance the customer journey, personalize interactions and deliver exceptional experiences.

- **Increase Revenue:** Will the change create new sources of revenue or boost sales? Evaluate the potential impact on sales growth, market expansion, product diversification or pricing strategies.

- **Reduced Costs:** Will the change lead to cost savings by improving processes or implementing automation? Assess the potential cost reductions through increased operational efficiency, resource optimization, or stream-lined workflows.

- **Increased Agility:** Will the change enhance the business's agility and responsiveness to market or industry changes? Consider how the change can enable faster decision-making, adaptability to evolving trends, and proactive responses to market shifts.

- **Potential Risks:** What are the potential risks associated with the change? Identify potential stakeholder resistance, challenges related to resource allocation or funding, operational disruptions, or any unforeseen consequences that may arise.

By thoroughly evaluating the benefits and risks of the change, you can develop strategies to maximize the positive outcomes and address potential challenges. This proactive approach will help you build a strong case for change and develop contingency plans to mitigate risks effectively.

Expected Results

In addition to determining the benefits and risks associated with the change, it is important to identify the expected results or outcomes in a clear and measurable way. This is where **SMART** objectives come in. **SMART** is an acronym that stands for Specific, Measurable, Achievable, Relevant, and Time-bound.

SMART objectives provide a framework for setting clear and meaningful goals that can guide the implementation process effectively.

- **Specific:** The expected results should be specific and well-defined. They should clearly state what is to be achieved, leaving no room for ambiguity or misinterpretation. This specificity helps stakeholders understand the intended outcomes and increases engagement by providing a clear direction.

- **Measurable:** The expected results should be measurable so that progress can be tracked and evaluated. Establishing quantifiable metrics or indicators allows for objective assessment and enables effective monitoring of the initiative. Measurable objectives provide a basis for measuring success and hold individuals and teams accountable for their performance.

- **Achievable:** The expected results should be realistic and attainable within the given resources, constraints, and timeline. Setting achievable objectives ensures that the change initiative remains feasible and increases the likelihood of successful implementation. It helps prevent setting unrealistic expectations and promotes a sense of confidence and motivation among stakeholders.

- **Relevant:** The expected results should be relevant and aligned with the overall objectives and strategic direction of the organization. They should contribute to the broader goals and vision of the organization, ensuring that the change initiative has a meaningful impact and value. By ensuring the relevance of objectives, organizations can maintain focus and prioritize efforts that directly contribute to desired outcomes.

- **Time-bound:** The expected results should be time-bound, meaning they should have a specific timeline or deadline for achievement. Setting time-bound objectives creates a sense of urgency, helps prioritize actions, and fosters accountability throughout the implementation process. Clear timelines provide a framework for planning, tracking progress, and holding individuals and teams accountable for meeting deadlines.

Some examples of expected results:

⇒ **Manufacturing Facility:** Improve the inventory management processes and achieve a 20% increase in efficiency within the first year of implementing the automated system.

⇒ **Small Business:** Reduce physical storage space by 50% within one year, eliminating the need for off-site storage.

⇒ **Solopreneur:** Acquire 20% more clients within six months through targeted marketing strategies and lead generation campaigns.

By identifying SMART objectives as part of the expected results, organizations can set clear targets for their change initiatives. These objectives serve as guiding principles, ensuring that the change remains focused, measurable, and aligned with the organization's strategic goals. They promote engagement by providing a sense of purpose and direction, and foster accountability by setting clear expectations, tracking progress, and celebrating achievements.

Assessing the Impact of Change

Another aspect of the change you need to consider are the different dimensions of the change. Change can have a significant impact on various areas of the organization, including:

- **People:** Roles, responsibilities, ways of working, and the mental and emotional well-being of individuals within the organization. It is important to assess how the change will affect employees, their job roles, and the support they may need to navigate through the transition.

- **Processes:** Decision-making procedures, service delivery methods, and approval processes may undergo changes or require adjustments to accommodate the new initiatives. Assessing the impact on processes helps in identifying areas for process improvement, streamlining operations, and ensuring efficient workflow.

- **Systems:** Technological infrastructure, tools, and equipment may need to be considered and potentially modified to support the change. This could involve implementing new software systems, upgrading hardware, or integrating various systems to enable seamless operations.

While you may not have all the details at this stage for a detailed assessment, you may consider various dimensions and elements that will be affected, such as:

- **Location(s):** Identify the specific locations where the change will take place. This could be a single location, multiple branches, or even global locations if the change has a wide reach. Understanding the geographical scope of the change helps in planning logistics, resource allocation, and communication strategies.

- **Functional area(s):** Determine the specific areas of the business that will be affected by the change. This could include departments such as finance, human resources, operations, marketing, and customer service, among others. By identifying the functional areas impacted, you can involve the relevant stakeholders and tailor change management activities accordingly.

- **Business process(es):** Identify the specific processes that will be affected by the change. This involves identifying the current processes and determining how they will be modified or replaced by the change initiative. Understanding the impact on business processes helps identify potential risks, opportunities for improvement, and areas that require specific attention during implementation.

- **Timing:** Identify the timeline for the change, which includes any project phases, and milestones. Consider the overall duration of the change initiative as well as the phased approach, if applicable. This will help you to effectively manage resources, set expectations, identify quick wins, and ensure timely completion of the change.

"Change's impact unfolds across people, processes, and systems. Assessing each dimension leads to tailored strategies that conquer challenges and embrace transformation."

Change in a Nutshell

In this stage, you will identify the change and the reasons for the change from a high-level perspective. By analyzing these aspects, you will acquire a comprehensive overview of the reasons for change, enabling stakeholders to understand the broader context and rationale behind the transformation. The insights obtained during this process will serve as a valuable tool for strategic decision-making, communication, and change management processes.

Change Scope Overview

- **Current State:** The current situation or process that needs to be changed.

- **Future State:** The desired end state or outcome that the change aims to achieve.

- **What is the change?** A specific description of the change that will occur.

- **Why is it needed?** The reason why the change is necessary and how it will address the problem or improve the situation.

- **What are the drivers of the Change? External/ Internal?** Factors or forces motivating, directing, or initiating the change.

   ◊ **External drivers** - market trends, customer demands, or regulatory requirements

   ◊ **Internal drivers** - goals, strategic initiatives, or process improvements.

- **How does it align with the vision?** How the proposed change is in harmony with the long-term goals, vision, mission, and strategic direction of the organization.

- **Benefits:** Anticipated benefits of the change, such as improved efficiency, cost savings, or increased customer satisfaction.

- **Risks:** Potential risks or challenges associated with the change and developing strategies to mitigate them.

- **Expected Results:** Clear and measurable statements of the outcomes or achievements expected from the change initiative, following the SMART (Specific, Measurable, Achievable, Relevant, Time-bound) framework.

- **Location(s):** Identify the specific locations where the change will take place.

- **Functional area(s):** Areas of the business that will be affected by the change.

- **Business process(es):** Specific processes that will be affected by the change.

- **Timing:** The timeline for the change, which includes any project phases, and milestones.

---

*Refer to **Section II** for **Toolkit**.* Please note that specific details may vary based on the context and requirements of your project or organization.

You can summarize the information of your change in the *Change Scope Overview* template included in the Toolkit Section.

By considering these elements, you can gain a holistic understanding of the change, and its purpose, to define the necessary steps for successful implementation. This knowledge lays the foundation for effective planning, stakeholder engagement, and overall strategy.

Identifying Stakeholders

Once you have a clear understanding of the change, it's important to identify the key stakeholders who impact or will be impacted by the change. Stakeholders are individuals and groups directly or indirectly affected by and capable of influencing a change effort.

Identifying key stakeholders is important because it helps you to understand their needs and concerns, anticipate potential roadblocks, and develop strategies to address these issues effectively.

These stakeholders may include employees, customers, partners, suppliers, community and other individuals or groups who have a vested interest in the success of the organization.

"Stakeholders hold the power to shape change. Engage them, understand their needs, and watch your transformation thrive."

Here are some of the types of who your stakeholders might be:

- **Internal stakeholders:** Think about those within your

organization who will be directly affected by the change. They can be your employees, managers, departments, and business units. Changes in roles, responsibilities or working conditions can have a direct impact on them.

- **External stakeholders:** Think about those outside your organization who will be directly affected by the change. They can be your customers, suppliers, partners, regulators, and the community. Changes in the delivery of products or services, as well as changes in the regulations that govern the organization can impact them.

- **Impacted stakeholders:** There are those who may be impacted by the change yet may not have a direct interest in it. An example of this is a change in the manufacturing process that may impact the local community, even if the latter may not have a direct interest in it.

- **Interested stakeholders:** These are individuals or groups who have an interest in the change but may not be directly affected by it. For example, shareholders may have an interest in a change that is expected to improve the financial performance of the organization.

If you want your change to become successful, make sure you identify and engage your stakeholders early and often. This helps you build trust, gain buy-in and ensure success of the initiative. It requires effective communication, active involvement and addressing concerns and feedback in a transparent and timely manner.

Sponsor

The Sponsor plays a key role in leading and supporting the change process. Typically, a senior executive or manager, the sponsor, champions the change initiative by communicating the vision and benefits of the change, securing necessary resources and support, and fostering a positive and inclusive culture throughout the process.

The Leadership Team, consisting of senior executives and managers, (where applicable) also plays a critical role in driving the change. They provide guidance, make strategic decisions, and ensure alignment with the organization's goals and objectives. Their active involvement and support are essential for successfully implementing the change and overcoming possible obstacles.

By actively involving and aligning stakeholders, sponsors, and the leadership team, organizations can create a collaborative and supportive environment that promotes the acceptance and adoption of the change. This collective effort increases the likelihood of achieving the desired outcomes and realizing the benefits of the change initiative.

Team

Selecting the right team to implement changes within an organization makes all the difference in achieving success in the change process. A well-chosen team can ensure that the change is implemented in a structured and efficient manner, while a poorly chosen team can lead to delays, confusion, and, ultimately, failure.

When assembling the project team, there are several factors to consider:

- **Expertise and Skills:** Select team members with the necessary expertise and skills to implement the change successfully. This includes knowledge of the specific change and the methodologies and tools required. Assessing and providing training as needed will enhance the team's competencies.

- **Diversity:** A diverse team can bring different perspectives and ideas to the table, which can help identify potential risks and opportunities that a homogeneous group may overlook.

- **Team Dynamics:** Effective communication and collaboration are significant contributors to a team's success. The team should possess good interpersonal skills and work well together, ensuring efficient and effective implementation of the change.

- **Availability:** Team members should be available to actively participate in the change process and dedicate sufficient time to complete their assigned tasks and responsibilities.

- **Commitment:** Your team members must also be committed to the change initiative and willing to take ownership of their roles in the process. They must be passionate about the initiative and committed to its success.

- **Leadership Support:** The team should have the support of the organization's leadership and stakeholders, as this support contributes to the success of the change initiative.

Once the team is assembled, you need to provide them with the necessary resources and support for their success. This includes training on the methodologies and tools to be used, establishing clear communication channels, and providing regular updates on the progress of the change.

Setting clear goals, timelines, metrics, and expectations is also important to keep the team focused and ensure they work efficiently toward implementing the change.

By carefully selecting and empowering the project team, you can strengthen their efforts and increase the opportunity for successful change implementation. The team's combined expertise, diverse perspectives, and strong collaboration will contribute to the effective execution of the change initiative.

Stakeholder List

The Stakeholder List will help you identify and understand the different interests, concerns, and needs of stakeholders. This includes understanding what motivates each stakeholder and how the change will impact them. The Interests section helps you identify and address the benefits and concerns relevant to each stakeholder group, allowing you to tailor your communication and engagement strategies accordingly.

⇒ A stakeholder from the sales department might be interested in increased revenue and improved sales processes due to the change. On the other hand, a stakeholder from the IT department may be concerned about the impact of the change on existing systems and the need for additional training or resources. By understanding these interests, you can craft messages and actions that speak directly to each stakeholder's motivations and address their specific needs and concerns.

The basic components of the **Stakeholder List** include:

- **Stakeholder Name:** The name or title of the individual, group, or organization that is considered a stakeholder.

- **Stakcholdcr Role:** The role or position that the stakeholder holds within the organization or in relation to the change initiative.

- **Stakeholder Classification:** This categorizes stakeholders as internal or external to the organization. Internal stakeholders are those directly associated with the organization, such as employees or managers, while external stakeholders include customers, suppliers, regulators, or community members.

- **Interests:** The interests, concerns and needs of the stakeholder, what's in it for me (WIIFM)?

- **Contact Information:** Contact details of the stakeholder, such as their email address, phone number, or any other relevant contact information.

Refer to **Section II** *for* **Toolkit**. Please note that specific details may vary based on the context and requirements of your project or organization.

You can summarize the information of your change in the **Stakeholder List** template included in Toolkit Section.

The basic components of the Stakeholder List serve as a foundation for identifying and organizing stakeholders. They provide a starting point for conducting a further stakeholder analysis, where additional components will be included to gather more comprehensive information about each stakeholder's influence, attitudes, and potential impact on the change initiative.

However, it is important to note that the Stakeholder List is not a static document. It should be regularly updated and reviewed throughout the change process to ensure it remains accurate and up to date. As more information becomes available and the change progresses, new stakeholders may emerge, while the level of influence and impact of existing stakeholders may change.

Leading the Change

Implementing changes within an organization requires strong and effective leadership. Leaders, including sponsors, must be prepared to guide their teams through the change process, communicate the benefits of the change, and address any challenges that arise.

To make this happen, you need to have a clear understanding of the goals of the change initiative and how it aligns with the overall vision of the organization. You must also be able to communicate these goals and vision to the team members and stakeholders and create a sense of urgency around the need for change.

Effective leadership requires:

- a clear understanding of the goals and vision,
- the ability to communicate these effectively,
- building a change team with the necessary skills and passion,
- involving stakeholders in the change process, and addressing resistance and challenges in a collaborative and solution-focused manner

Now that you have defined the change and identified the stakeholders, it's time to move on to the next step: developing a strategy for implementing the change. This involves completing a detailed change impact assessment and creating a roadmap that outlines the specific actions, resources, and timelines required to achieve your goals.

In **Step 2: Develop the Strategy**, we will explore how to develop an effective strategy customized to suit the specific objectives and requirements of your organization. As you conclude the initial phase of your change journey, take a moment to appreciate the foundation you have built by defining the change. The next step holds the key to help you transform your vision into reality, as you unleash your strategic ability and create a roadmap toward your goals.

Define the Change

STEP 1

THINGS TO REMEMBER:

- Clearly define desired outcomes and objectives.

- Understand the nature, scope, and specific changes required.

- Identify reasons and motivations driving the need for change.

- Ensure the change aligns with long-term goals and strategic direction.

- Evaluate potential benefits and risks, setting realistic and measurable targets.

- Analyze the impact of the change.

- Identify key stakeholders.

- Secure sponsorship and support from key leaders.

- Assemble a dedicated and capable team.

- Provide effective leadership to create a supportive environment for change.

- Summarize the essence of the change in a concise manner.

Going Paperless: Electronic Batch Record Project

In Step 1, we embarked on the journey of going paperless with the Electronic Batch Record project. This specific change initiative focuses on transforming our organization's processes in the areas of people, processes, and systems. To ensure the success of this initiative, a cross-functional team consisting of operators, supervisors, and support personnel from Quality, Document Management, IT, Engineering, and other relevant departments was formed. This team was backed by strong leadership and sponsorship, ensuring effective collaboration and seamless execution.

One of the key considerations during this phase was defining the project scope and objectives. The team carefully identified the specific processes and areas that would be affected by the transition to a paperless system. By clearly outlining the objectives of the project, such as improving data accuracy, enhancing record accessibility, and reducing manual errors, we set a clear direction for the implementation.

Recognizing the importance of proper preparation, we provided extensive training to the team, equipping them with the necessary knowledge and skills in the approach and methodology required for successful implementation. As part of our initial assessment, we conducted a Scope Overview of the Changes across all areas, laying the groundwork for the development of a comprehensive strategy that encompasses the entire change process.

Furthermore, throughout Step 1, we actively engaged key stakeholders who have a direct or indirect influence on the change initiative. These stakeholders include project team members, operators, supervisors, and support areas such as Quality and Document Management. Additionally, we involved other stakeholders who play crucial roles in the Process and Systems aspects of the project.

By defining the scope of changes and involving stakeholders from diverse areas, we have set a solid foundation for a successful implementation. Now, as we proceed to **Step 2: Develop the Strategy**, our focus will be on developing the strategy specifically tailored to our objectives and requirements.

Let us continue our journey and transform our vision of going paperless into a tangible reality.

Step 2
Develop the Strategy

"A clear strategy empowers you to make decisions with confidence and purpose."

In the previous step, you have gained a comprehensive understanding of the need for change, its potential impact, and the stakeholders involved. With this acquired knowledge, you will now embark on the task of developing a clear and well-thought-out strategy to guide the change process. This step focuses on the "how" and "when" of change implementation and complements the activities that take place in the planning phase of a project.

Strategize: Plan and Align

Preparing for change involves planning a strategy that outlines how resources will be utilized to achieve the defined objectives. The strategy encompasses a range of elements, including processes, metrics, behaviors, tools, systems, skills, and techniques that are essential for successful change implementation.

It is important to consider that the choice of strategy depends on the specific change and the unique characteristics of your organization. The strategy will be influenced by the assessments conducted, along with the level of risk associated with the change. A large-scale radical change in a change-resistant organization will require comprehensive planning and greater effort, while a smaller change within a specific department may call for a more streamlined approach.

Remember that no matter the size of the change, you still should apply this methodology – these steps – with your team. Doing this will enhance their change competencies, preparing your organization for ongoing success.

Changes can cause disruptions and require employees, customers, or end users to learn new skills and adapt to new ways of working or routines. As a result, you either need to, **implement new systems and processes, upgrade or redesign existing ones, or discard outdated and obsolete ones**.

Various aspects of an organization can be impacted, including:

- **Technology:** Upgrading to new software, implementing a new CRM system or changing internet service providers can require employees to adapt to new systems, learn new features and interfaces, and transfer data.

- **Operations:** Adopting a new business model or a change in a product line can require employees to adapt to new ways of working and new processes.

- **Financial systems:** Adapting to a change in revenue or a change in expenses can affect a company's budget, savings, and financial goals. This may require the company to utilize new financial systems and tools, such as budgeting apps or financial forecasting.

- **Human resources:** Managing a change in the company's workforce such as layoffs or new hires, can affect the company's payroll and benefits systems.

- **Supply Chain:** Adjusting to a change in the company's production or distribution can affect its logistics, inventory management and procurement systems.

By following a structured process for developing the strategy, you will benefit from the enhanced direction, focus, and alignment of resources and activities. The strategy will serve as a guiding framework for decision-making, helping to keep change efforts on track and ensuring that the desired outcomes are achieved.

Remember, every change initiative is unique, and the size and risk level of the change will influence your approach. By conducting a preliminary evaluation, you can determine the level of effort and detail required to create a robust plan. Whether you are embarking on a transformative change in a large organization or implementing a small-scale change within a specific group, this chapter will provide you with the tools needed to develop an effective strategy.

"A well-crafted strategy acts as a compass, guiding resources and activities towards defined objectives in the face of change."

Business Process Review

Every change in an organization may impact processes in one way or another. Changes can affect the processes and systems (technology, tools, equipment) used to carry out day-to-day activities, the way work is done, the way decisions are made, and the way services are delivered.

These changes can manifest in various ways, including technology upgrades, operational shifts, financial system modifications, human resource adjustments, and supply chain transformations. To effectively navigate these changes, integrating business process tools can greatly assist in developing a comprehensive change strategy. These tools help identify opportunities for automation, standardization, and simplification.

After understanding the high-level change to be implemented, as described in Step 1, the next step is to review the detailed processes and identify specific gaps between the current and future states. This activity is critical to complete the detailed change impact assessment.

The purpose of the business process review is to identify potential gaps between the current and the future state of the processes. This analysis allows for a deeper understanding of how changes may impact various aspects of the organization, including employees, customers, and systems. By pin-pointing areas for improvement, the review sets the stage for enhancing the efficiency and effectiveness of processes.

In this area, you must follow a structured business process management approach to analyze, design and or improve business processes. There are different approaches to map the business processes (Lean, BPM, system related, among others). The decision is yours to select the one that suits your needs. The important thing is to complete the business process review.

By incorporating these principles into the strategy, you can ensure that the change efforts are aligned with the business processes, leading to more efficient and effective outcomes.

To complete the change strategy, consider the following key activities:

Current State: AS IS

- Identify and assess the **business processes** and **systems** that need to be changed.

- Analyze the **current state** of the business processes and identify areas for improvement.

- Understand the current **metrics and systems** (technology, tools, equipment) in place to support the processes and operations and identify where changes are needed.

Future State: TO BE

- Design **new processes** to support the change.

- Create **process flow diagrams**, including **metrics**, and specify process **roles and responsibilities**.

- Identify any new **systems or technologies** that may be needed to support the new processes.

CHANGE

- Assess the **impact of the change** on the business processes and systems.

- Determine which **processes** need to be redesigned or modified to support the change.

- Specify the areas of the processes and systems that will be impacted by the change, including changes to **technology, tools, and equipment** used or changes to the way systems are configured or operated.

- Understand the potential impact of the change on **people, efficiency, effectiveness**, and security of the processes and systems.

Participation of project team members and business process owners is critical for the success of this activity and the overall strategy. Their input and expertise ensure a comprehensive review and assessment of business processes, leading to more efficient and effective outcomes.

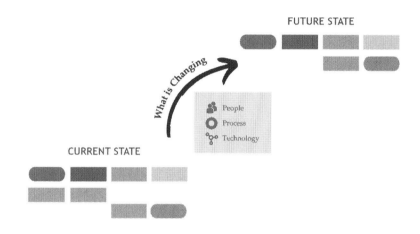

By following a structured business process review approach, you can ensure that your change initiatives are aligned with your business processes, leading to a more seamless and successful implementation. It provides a systematic approach for assessing, mapping, and improving processes, enabling informed decision-making and the development of strategies that optimize operations and drive positive change.

Once business process reviews are completed, each team will have a comprehensive list of proposed changes by area or process. Now, the team can identify the metrics to effectively measure and assess the progress.

Performance Metrics and Targets

By establishing clear and measurable indicators at this stage, you lay the foundation for tracking progress and measuring the success of your change efforts. Performance metrics provide quantifiable measures that reflect the desired outcomes, while targets set specific goals to strive for. These metrics and targets ensure that you have a solid framework for evaluating the effectiveness of your change initiative and provide valuable insights for making data-driven decisions throughout the implementation process.

In Step 1, you gained valuable insights from the change scope overview. Now, in Step 2, setting performance metrics and targets will allow you to align your objectives with measurable outcomes. This ensures that the metrics focus on tracking progress and determining whether the change initiative is moving in the right direction to deliver the intended benefits.

When setting performance metrics and targets, it's important to ensure that they directly align with the expected outcomes identified in Step 1. This alignment ensures that the metrics are focused on measuring the desired results and progress toward achieving them. By linking the metrics to the expected outcomes, you create a clear path for assessing whether the change initiative is moving in the right direction and delivering the intended benefits.

For example, if one of the expected results identified in Step 1 is to improve operational efficiency, a performance metric could be the cycle time of a key business process. By setting a target to reduce the cycle time by 20% within the fiscal year, you establish a specific and measurable goal that reflects the desired outcome of increased efficiency.

Here are some additional examples of performance metrics and targets that can be set to help achieve the expected results identified in Step 1. These examples follow the SMART framework:

Performance Metrics Examples:

Improve Operational Efficiency – measure **Cycle Time Reduction** in days

⇒ Reduce the cycle time by 20% within six months

Increase Employee Engagement – use surveys or assessments to measure **Employee Engagement** Score

⇒ Increase the engagement score by 15% within one year.

Enhance Product Quality – measure **Defect Rate** in percentage of defective products

⇒ Reduce the defect rate to less than 1% of total production within six months

Improve Service Response Time – measure **Average Response Time** in minutes or hours

⇒ Decrease the average response time to customer inquiries to under 24 hours within three months

Enhance Sales Performance – measure **Sales Conversion Rate** in percentage of leads converted to sales

⇒ Increase the sales conversion rate by 20% within the next quarter

Optimize Supply Chain – measure **Order Fulfillment Cycle Time** in days or hours

⇒ Reduce the order fulfillment cycle time by 30% within the fiscal year

Improve Customer Retention – measure **Customer Retention Rate** in percentage of customers retained over a specific period

⇒ Achieve a customer retention rate of 90% within six months

These examples illustrate how performance metrics and targets can be tailored to specific objectives identified in Step 1. By setting these metrics and targets, you provide a quantifiable way to track progress, measure the impact of the change, and make informed decisions based on data-driven insights. This ensures that your change initiatives remain on track and aligned with the strategic goals and priorities of the organization.

Change Impact Assessment

After conducting a thorough business process review in this step, it is now possible to get into the specific details of the change and its impact on various aspects of the organization. The **Change Impact Assessment** is an important deliverable that builds upon the **Change Scope Overview** conducted previously.

By understanding the impact of the change, you can develop a comprehensive plan for achieving your goals and mitigate potential risks. This assessment enables you to identify the optimal strategy, allocate necessary resources, and secure the support required for successful implementation. It also allows you and your team to make informed decisions, minimize risks and disruptions, gain stakeholder support, and maximize the benefits of the change.

Benefits, when you conduct a change impact assessment, include:

- **Improved decision-making:** Weigh the pros and cons and determine the best way to implement the change.

- **Mitigated risks:** Develop risk-mitigating strategies, implement contingency plans, and adjust timelines.

- **Increased buy-in and support:** Understand the needs and concerns of stakeholders for better commitment.

- **Enhanced communication:** Facilitate the constant flow of valuable information, ensuring that stakeholders are aligned and informed.

- **Reduced disruptions:** Identify potential delays, productivity issues, market volatility, and resistance to change.

- **Improved training and development:** Tailor programs to address the knowledge and skill gaps of affected stakeholders.

Adopting an assessment-driven approach positions you with a solid foundation for successful change implementation, leading your organization or business toward growth.

Major Components of the Change Impact Assessment

- **Assess the Change:** Understand the specific changes that will be implemented in different areas of the organization.

- **Analyze the Impact:** Analyze the potential impact of the change on people, processes, systems, and resources. Identify the areas that will be directly or indirectly affected and evaluate the extent of the impact.

- **Identify Stakeholders:** Identify the individuals or groups who will be affected by the change and determine their level of involvement. Consider stakeholders from different departments, levels of the organization, and external entities.

- **Assess Risk and Benefits:** Determine and evaluate the benefit and risks associated with the change. Identify the positive outcomes and leverage them. Assess the potential negative consequences and develop strategies to mitigate them.

It is recommended that each area identified as part of the change conduct a detailed impact assessment. During this process, the change is assessed from different perspectives. For example, in the case of going paperless, detailed assessments would be performed on weigh dispensing, document management, manufacturing execution and product release processes. Each area would be impacted in different ways, from the physical activities to people's knowledge and system support.

Key components of the Change Impact Assessment include:

- **Functional Area** - Identify the specific areas of the business that will be affected by the change. Determine how the change will impact departments, teams, and individuals within the organization.

- **Business Process** - Enlist the specific processes that will be affected by the change. Assess how the change will influence the workflow, roles and responsibilities, and overall efficiency of these processes.

- **Description of the Change** - Define the change. Provide a detailed explanation of the specific changes that will be implemented and affect stakeholders in different areas of the organization.

- **Level of Change Impact (People/Process/Systems)** - Assess the impact that the change will have on the functional areas based on its nature, such as people, process or systems. How the change will affect the specific functional area, ranging from high to low impact.

- **Location** - Confirm the specific locations where the change will take place. Determine if the change will impact certain physical locations, branches, or offices within the organization.

- **Departments Impacted** - Identify the specific departments or teams that will be affected by the change. Understand the organizational structure and identify the areas that will undergo significant changes.

- **Roles Impacted** - Validate the specific roles or positions that will be affected by the change. Determine how the change will impact job responsibilities and reporting relationships.

- **Number of People Impacted** - Estimate the number of people who will be affected by the change. Understand the scale of impact on the workforce and the resources needed to support them through the transition.

- **Timing** - Specify the timing or duration when the change needs to be implemented. Take into consideration if there is a phased approach.

- **Benefits** - Identify the potential benefits that can be realized through the change. Assess the positive impacts on productivity, customer satisfaction, cost reduction, or other relevant areas.

- **Risks** - Assess potential risks or challenges associated with the change to develop strategies to mitigate them. Evaluate the possible negative consequences to devise plans to address them effectively.

Refer to **Section II** *for* **Toolkit.** Please note that specific details may vary based on the context and requirements of your project or organization.

You can summarize the information of your change in the *Change Impact Assessment* template included in Toolkit Section.

The results of the Change Impact Assessment provide valuable insights for decision-making and formulating strategies to manage the change effectively. It supports the stakeholder analysis, communications, training needs and helps organizations and individuals anticipate potential challenges, mitigate risks, and maximize the benefits of the change.

Stakeholder Management

In Step 1 – Define the Change – you have already compiled an initial list of stakeholders, considering both internal and external stakeholders and assessing their interests in relation to the change. However, as you progress through the Change Impact Assessment, more information and details about the change become available, making it necessary to update the stakeholder list accordingly. The primary objective remains the same: to identify all stakeholders, gain a comprehensive understanding of their interests, and evaluate how the change may impact them.

By involving stakeholders early in the process, you can increase the likelihood of achieving your goals and creating positive outcomes for everyone involved. Building buy-in and support from stakeholders during the initial phases of the change can generate support, reduce resistance, and improve your chances of success. This inclusive approach establishes effective communication, fosters a sense of shared responsibility and ownership, and ensures that the change is well-received by all parties involved.

"The timely engagement of stakeholders enhances goal attainment, fosters support, and mitigates resistance."

Once stakeholders have been identified, you need to assess the impact of the change on each stakeholder group. This involves the identification of the potential benefits and risks that the change presents for each group, along with the evaluation of their support or resistance toward the change. By conducting these assessments, you gain valuable insights that help determine which stakeholders to engage with and how to engage them effectively.

By understanding stakeholders' interests and considering the potential impact of the change on each group, you can tailor your communication and engagement strategies to address their specific needs and concerns. This targeted approach will foster greater stakeholder involvement, build trust, and increase the likelihood of their support throughout the change process.

Regularly reviewing and updating the stakeholder list as more information becomes available ensures that your stakeholder management efforts remain comprehensive and responsive to the evolving needs of the change initiative. It allows you to effectively engage stakeholders, build relationships, address their concerns, and align their interests with the objectives of the change.

By actively involving stakeholders and considering their interests and potential impact, you create an environment that values their input, promotes collaboration, and significantly increases the likelihood of successful change implementation. This collaborative approach sets the foundation for effective stakeholder management and paves the way for a smoother and more successful change journey.

"Stakeholder management is the bridge that connects the aspirations of change with the reality of implementation, fostering a path towards tangible and impactful outcomes."

Understanding Stakeholders Perspectives

To effectively engage stakeholders, you must understand their perspectives on the change. This requires considering their interests, concerns, and any potential challenges or opportunities that the change may bring for them.

Once you have gained insights into the perspectives of stakeholders, the next step is to identify how the change will specifically impact each stakeholder. This analysis encompasses not only the immediate impacts but also the long-term effects that the change may have on each stakeholder group.

Based on the stakeholder analysis, a comprehensive plan is necessary to address stakeholder concerns and mitigate any negative impacts of the change. This plan may involve communication strategies, training programs, or other initiatives aimed at helping stakeholders adapt to the change effectively.

By conducting a stakeholder analysis, you can ensure that the strategy considers the perspectives and concerns of all those affected by the change, leading to a more successful implementation process.

With a clear understanding of the potential impact of the change on each stakeholder group, you can prioritize your engagement efforts. This includes identifying the groups that are most critical to the success of the change and recognizing the groups that may display resistance. It is important to engage with the critical stakeholders and address the concerns and resistance of other stakeholders.

Once you have completed the stakeholder assessment, you can add communication strategies to each stakeholder based on their level of impact and influence. These strategies will help ensure effective communication and engagement throughout the change process, fostering support and collaboration.

By understanding and addressing stakeholder perspectives, organizations can build strong relationships, foster trust, and increase the likelihood of stakeholder support and commitment to the change initiative. This approach creates a positive environment for change, where stakeholders feel heard, valued and included in the process.

Impact and Influence

In stakeholder management, understanding the impact and influence of stakeholders plays a huge factor in effective communication and engagement.

Impact refers to the degree to which a stakeholder is directly **affected by the change**. This includes both immediate and long-term effects on their roles, responsibilities, and work processes. Stakeholders with high impact are those who experience significant changes in their day-to-day activities, as a result of the change, while those with low impact may have minimal disruption.

⇒ In a company-wide restructuring, frontline employees who directly work in the affected departments may experience a high impact. Their roles, reporting relationships, and job responsibilities may undergo significant changes.

⇒ On the other hand, employees in non-affected departments may have low impact, with minimal changes to their daily work.

Influence, on the other hand, relates to a stakeholder's **ability to shape or sway decisions and outcomes**. Stakeholders with high influence have the power, authority, or expertise to drive change, whereas those with low influence may have limited decision-making authority or lesser influence over the overall process.

⇒ Senior executives and key department heads often possess high influence due to their decision-making authority and leadership roles. They can shape the direction of the change, allocate resources, and influence the organization's response to the change.

⇒ Conversely, individual contributors may have low influence in terms of decision-making power but can still provide valuable input and feedback.

Recognizing the levels of impact and influence among stakeholders allows you to design targeted communication strategies that address specific needs and concerns. By tailoring your communication approaches accordingly, you can enhance stakeholder engagement and increase the likelihood of their support and commitment to the change initiative. Understanding the varying degrees of impact and influence helps you customize your communication efforts, ensuring that you address the right stakeholders in the right way.

By integrating the insights from stakeholder perspectives, impact assessment, and influence evaluation, you can develop a holistic approach to stakeholder management. This comprehensive understanding of stakeholders' interests, concerns, impact, and influence allows you to create effective communication and engagement strategies that foster collaboration, build trust, and drive the success of the change initiative.

Stakeholder Analysis

The Stakeholder Analysis serves as a valuable tool for systematically identifying and understanding stakeholders, assessing their level of impact and influence, and developing tailored strategies to engage and manage their involvement in the change process. It provides a structured approach to stakeholder management, ensuring that their interests and concerns are effectively addressed, and their support is gained throughout the change initiative.

The Stakeholder Analysis template is created from the Stakeholder List created in Step 1. It has additional elements that complements the information already gathered.

- **Stakeholder Name -** Identify the individual, group, or organization involved as a stakeholder in the project or change.

- **Roles (s) -** Specify the stakeholder's role(s) in relation to the project or change, including team members and management.

- **Stakeholder Classification -** Determine if the stakeholder is internal or external to the organization or company.

- **Interests (WIIFM - /What's in it for me?) -** Outline the stakeholder's interests, concerns and potential benefits or impacts related to the change.

- **Level of Impact** - Assess the stakeholder's direct impact by the change on a scale of high (H), medium (M), or low (L)

- **Level of Influence** - Evaluate the stakeholder's influence over the project or change on a scale of high (H), medium (M), or low (L)

- **Desired Level of Support** - Specify the expected level of commitment from the stakeholder on a scale of high (H), medium (M), or low (L).

- **Current Level of Support** - Determine the stakeholder's present level of commitment to the change on the scale presented formerly.

- **Contact Information** - Identify the stakeholder's contact details, such as email address or phone number.

Refer to **Section II** *for* **Toolkit**. Please note that specific details may vary based on the context and requirements of your project or organization.

You can summarize the information of your change in the *Stakeholder Analysis* template included in Toolkit Section.

Once you complete the stakeholder analysis, you can identify communication strategies by each stakeholder group. You can add a column on the Stakeholder Analysis Template for additional references.

Communication Strategy

After acquiring a comprehensive understanding of stake-holders and their levels of influence, impact, and support for the change, it's time to harness the power of effective communication. Developing a well-crafted communication strategy that engages and informs stakeholders is the key to success.

A robust communication strategy ensures that the right messages reach the right stakeholders at the right time, fostering understanding, buy-in, and support throughout the change process. It bridges the gap between stakeholder analysis and successful change implementation, enabling the development and execution of effective communication strategies.

Tactics for Effective Communication

- Identify the Audience
- Develop Clear Objectives
- Tailor Messages to Different Audiences
- Utilize Multiple Channels
- Provide Regular Updates
- Encourage Two-Way Communication

In the fast-paced world of change, effective communication is key to bringing people together, aligning their efforts, and driving organizations toward their desired goals. It serves as a powerful tool to connect, inspire, and engage people. When implementing change, the role of communication becomes even more obvious – it needs an appropriate time for planning.

At its core, the communication strategy is all about engagement. It is the roadmap that guides us in navigating the complex terrain of change, ensuring that every message resonates, every interaction inspires, and every effort leads to meaningful action. By implementing a well-structured communication strategy, organizations can effectively manage resistance, address concerns, and foster stakeholder support for the change. The strategy encompasses key elements such as the messages to be conveyed, the target audience, communication methods and channels, a communication schedule, and a plan for measuring communication effectiveness.

Effective communication considers three essential components:

- what is said, (message)

- engaging the audience, and

- when it is said.

What is said involves providing stakeholders with clear and concise information about the change, emphasizing the benefits it will bring and the impact it will have on the organization and individuals. Transparency and honesty are vital in explaining the reasons behind the change in a manner that stakeholders can easily understand, as well as the benefits it will bring and the impact it will have on the organization and individual stakeholders.

What is said?

- Reasons for change
- Alignment with vision and strategy
- Benefits
- Risks of not changing
- What's In It For Me? WIIFM

When proposing a change, it is important to clearly communicate the benefits to those affected. This involves addressing the question of "What's in it for me?" or WIIFM. How will the change contribute towards improved performance, cost savings, increased competitiveness, enhanced customer satisfaction, improved employee satisfaction, compliance with regulations, or better alignment with personal or organizational values? Depending on the specific change and context, the benefits may vary, but they should always be communicated in a manner that resonates with stakeholders.

Initial communications should focus on creating awareness of the business reasons for change and the risks associated with not changing, keeping the messages high-level and avoiding distractions. These messages should be clear, concise, consistent, and address the reasons for the change, the benefits, and the impact on both the organization and individual stakeholders.

Some messages may include:

For **Employees** most directly impacted:

- Build support, mitigate resistance and communicate reasons for the change.

- Address concerns about job security and provide training and support to help employees adapt.

For **Customers** impacted by changes to products, services or processes:

- Encourage continued loyalty, communicate changes and address any concerns they may have.

- Provide education and support to help customers adapt or offer incentives.

For **Partners & Suppliers** impacted by changes to processes or relationships:

- Mitigate any potential issues, communicate changes and work collaboratively.

- Explore new opportunities for collaboration, renegotiate contracts, and provide training and support.

For the broader **Community** that may also be impacted in which the organization operates:

- To help community members adapt, communicate the benefits of the change.

- Support local initiatives or provide education and resources.

Having a clear **champion** for the change along with the support of leaders and key decision-makers can greatly contribute to successful implementation. The senders of the communication can vary depending on the messages and audience. Supervisors can address how the change will impact their group or day-to-day responsibilities, while executive leaders can communicate the business reasons for the change, how it aligns with the organization's vision and strategy, and the risks of not changing.

Moreover, **engaging the audience** is not a one-time event; it is an ongoing journey. The communication plan ensures that every step of the way, stakeholders receive the right information, at the right time, through the right channels. It provides a platform for continuous dialogue, updates, and collaboration, ensuring that everyone remains on the same page and moving in the same direction.

This includes providing opportunities for stakeholders to ask questions, give feedback, and share concerns. Regular updates on the progress, along with addressing concerns and questions, and actively involving stakeholders help build buy -in, commitment, and address resistance.

Communication Strategies by Level of Impact and Influence

Each communication strategy should be tailored to the specific needs, characteristics, and dynamics of the stakeholders and the change initiative. Flexibility, adaptability, and responsiveness are essential in implementing these strategies to ensure effective communication and stakeholder engagement.

The following communication strategies are designed as guidelines to align with different levels of impact and influence. By leveraging these strategies, you can build strong relationships, foster collaboration, and ensure stakeholders are well-informed and engaged throughout the change process. Let's explore the strategies for each level:

High Impact / High Influence:

Stakeholders in this category play a critical role in the change initiative, as they have a significant impact on its outcomes and possess substantial influence within the organization.

⇒ A high-level Business Leader of the company has a deep understanding of the change initiative and has the authority to make key decisions. They can influence the direction and implementation of the change, and their support is crucial for its success.

To effectively engage these stakeholders, proactive and collaborative communication strategies are essential. This includes involving them in decision-making processes, building strong relationships, and providing regular updates while seeking their input and feedback.

The following communication strategies can be employed:

- **Proactive Engagement:** Initiate frequent and direct communication with these stakeholders to keep them informed about the change, its objectives, and progress.

- **Collaborative Decision-Making:** Involve them in key decision-making processes and seek their expertise and insights to ensure their buy-in and commitment.

- **Tailored Communication:** Customize communication messages to address their specific interests, concerns, and needs, highlighting the benefits and impacts that are relevant to them.

- **Two-Way Communication:** Create opportunities for open dialogue, feedback, and questions. Actively listen to their perspectives and address any challenges or barriers they may identify.

- **Personalized Engagement:** Provide individual attention and support to these stakeholders, recognizing their influence and valuing their contributions.

- **Leadership Alignment:** Ensure that senior leaders are actively involved in the communication process, demonstrating their support and commitment to the change.

High Impact/High Influence Stakeholders

Gain their support and leverage their expertise to drive the change.

High Impact / Low Influence:

These stakeholders are highly impacted by the change but may not have significant influence over it. Although they may not have the power to shape the change, their understanding and support are crucial for its successful implementation.

⇒ Frontline employees who are directly affected by the change but may not have the power to influence the decision-making process. They have a strong interest in understanding how the change will affect their day-to-day work and may require support and training to adapt to the new processes.

To build their understanding and support, the following communication strategies can be employed:

- **Clear and Transparent Communication:** Provide clear and concise information about the change, its objectives, and the reasons behind it. Be transparent about the impacts and benefits that the change will bring.

- **Education and Awareness:** Conduct training sessions, workshops, or informational sessions to enhance their understanding of the change and its implications.

- **Demonstrating the WIIFM (What's in it for me?):** Emphasize the personal benefits and positive outcomes that the change will bring for these stakeholders.

- **Building Supportive Coalitions:** Identify influential stakeholders who have a strong relationship with these stakeholders and leverage their support and endorsement to build credibility and acceptance.

- **Addressing Concerns:** Actively listen to their concerns and questions. Provide timely and honest responses, addressing their specific worries and uncertainties.

- **Feedback Mechanisms:** Establish channels for them to share their feedback, suggestions, and concerns. Regularly gather their input to ensure their voices are heard and considered.

High Impact/Low Influence Stakeholders

Address their concerns and emphasize the benefits of the change for them.

Low Impact / High Influence:

Stakeholders in this category may not be directly impacted by the change, but their influence is significant. To gain their support and active involvement, it is important to highlight the broader organizational or strategic benefits of the change and engage them in decision-making processes. Recognizing their contributions and demonstrating appreciation will further reinforce their engagement.

⇒ External consultants who possess specialized knowledge and expertise may not be directly impacted by the change. Their influence lies in providing recommendations and guidance to the organization based on their expertise, which can shape the direction of the change.

To effectively engage low impact/high influence stakeholders, the following communication strategies can be employed:

- **Influencer Engagement:** Identify and engage key influencers who have a strong relationship with these stakeholders. Leverage their support and influence to advocate for the change and create a positive perception among their peers.

- **Communicating Strategic Alignment:** Emphasize how the change aligns with the organization's strategic goals, vision, or mission, highlighting its relevance and importance in the broader context.

- **Creating a Sense of Ownership:** Engage these stakeholders in shaping the change by involving them in decision-making processes or seeking their input on specific aspects of the change.

- **Highlighting Leadership Support:** Ensure that senior leaders demonstrate their support and commitment to the change, reinforcing its importance and value.

- **Leveraging Networks:** Utilize existing networks or forums where these stakeholders have the influence to share information, gather support, and address any resistance.

- **Recognition and Appreciation:** Acknowledge their contributions and efforts in supporting the change, highlighting their influence and the positive impact they can have on its success.

Low Impact/High Influence Stakeholders

Align their interests with the broader organizational goals. Gain their support and involvement.

Low Impact / Low Influence:

For stakeholders in this category, it is important to keep them informed and engaged, even though they may have limited impact and influence. Regular updates, opportunities for feedback, and recognition of their contributions must be provided. It should focus on the specific impacts that affect them directly. This will foster a sense of involvement and ensure their perspectives are considered.

⇒**Non-operational staff** who may have minimal impact on

the change and limited influence within the organization can still benefit from staying informed about the change and providing feedback or suggestions if needed.

To effectively engage low impact/low influence stakeholders, the following communication strategies can be employed:

- **Clear and Concise Communication:** Provide essential information about the change in a clear, concise, and accessible manner, focusing on the impacts that may directly affect them.

- **Regular Updates:** Share periodic updates on the progress of the change to keep them informed and engaged, even if their involvement is limited.

- **Demonstrating Relevance:** Highlight how the change connects to the broader organizational goals or the work they are involved in, showcasing the value and relevance of the change to their role or responsibilities.

- **Opportunities for Feedback:** Offer channels for them to provide feedback, ask questions, or share any concerns they may have. Demonstrate that their input is valued and considered.

- **Recognition and Appreciation:** Acknowledge their support and contributions, even if they have limited involvement, to foster a sense of belonging and engagement.

- **Utilize Existing Communication Channels:** Leverage

existing communication channels within the organization, such as newsletters, intranet, or team meetings, to reach these stakeholders effectively.

Low Impact/Low Influence Stakeholders

Keep them informed and ensure their perspectives are considered.

By implementing these communication strategies, tailored to the specific needs and concerns of stakeholders, you can enhance stakeholder engagement, foster collaboration, address their perspectives, build support for the change initiative and increase the chances of a successful implementation.

Timing

Equally important as the content of the communication is the timing of when it is delivered. To ensure effective stakeholder engagement, you need to share the right messages at the right time throughout the change process. Timely communication helps keep stakeholders informed, addresses concerns promptly, and provides them with the necessary information to adapt to the change.

The communication plan plays a vital role in guiding the timing of communication efforts. It outlines the schedule of regular updates, milestones, and key touchpoints with stakeholders. By adhering to the plan, you can ensure that communication is delivered consistently and in a timely manner.

Communication Channels

One important aspect of timing is selecting the appropriate communication channels for different messages and target audiences. Different channels offer varying levels of immediacy, interactivity, and reach.

Some Communication Channels

- Conference Calls
- Interactive Meetings
- Newsletter
- Social Media
- Emails
- SharePoint/Websites

The choice of communication channels should be based on the preferences and accessibility of your stakeholders, as well as the nature of the message you want to convey. Using a combination of different channels can help ensure that you reach a wider audience, cater to different communication preferences, and maximize stakeholder engagement throughout the change process.

Here are some examples of communication channels commonly used:

- **Conference Calls:** Virtual meetings that allow stakeholders to participate remotely and discuss key topics or updates.

- **Interactive Meetings:** In-person or virtual meetings that provide a platform for stakeholders to engage in discussions, ask questions, and provide feedback.

- **Newsletters:** Periodic publications that deliver updates, highlights, and relevant information in a concise and accessible format.

- **Social Media:** Platforms such as Twitter, LinkedIn, or internal social networks that facilitate real-time communication, announcements, and discussions.

- **Emails:** Direct and personalized messages that can be used for targeted communication, sharing important updates, or addressing specific stakeholder concerns.

- **SharePoint/Websites:** Online platforms where stakeholders can access resources, documents, and updates related to the change initiative.

- **Town Hall Meetings:** Large-scale meetings where stakeholders have the opportunity to directly interact with key leaders, ask questions, and provide feedback.

- **Webinars:** Online seminars or presentations that allow stakeholders to participate remotely, learn about the change initiative, and engage in interactive discussions.

- **One-on-One Meetings:** Individual meetings with stakeholders to address their specific concerns, gather feedback, and provide personalized support.

- **Focus Groups:** Small, representative groups of stakeholders who come together to share their opinions, experiences, and suggestions regarding the change initiative.

- **Surveys and Feedback Forms:** Online or offline questionnaires designed to gather structured feedback and opinions from stakeholders, allowing for anonymity and honest responses.

- **Project Collaboration Tools:** Online platforms that facilitate collaboration, document sharing, and discussion among stakeholders involved in the change initiative.

- **Video Presentations:** Recorded or live videos that convey key messages, provide updates, or share success stories related to the change initiative.

When determining the timing of communication, consider the urgency and importance of the message, the stakeholder's preferred mode of communication, and the accessibility of the chosen channels.

By incorporating the right timing into your communication plan and utilizing appropriate communication channels, you can maximize the effectiveness of your stakeholder engagement efforts and create a conducive environment for successful change implementation.

Communication Plan

A well-structured communication plan is essential for effectively conveying your messages to stakeholders and ensuring a smooth implementation of change. By considering key elements within your communication plan, you can create a strategic framework that guides your communication efforts and maximizes stakeholder engagement.

The communication plan elements outlined below provide a comprehensive approach to developing your communication strategy:

Communication Plan Elements:

- **Channel** – Determine the most effective communication channels or vehicles to deliver your messages to stakeholders. This can include face-to-face meetings, emails, newsletters, intranet, social media platforms, webinars, or town hall meetings.

- **Objectives** – Clearly define the goals and outcomes that the communication aims to achieve. These objectives can include creating awareness, fostering understanding, addressing concerns, generating support, and promoting collaboration.

- **Key Messages** - The core messages that need to be

conveyed to stakeholders, aligned with the purpose of the change. They should communicate the benefits, rationale, and impact of the change.

- **Audience** - The specific individuals or stakeholder groups who will receive the communication. This can include employees, managers, executives, customers, suppliers, shareholders, or any other relevant parties.

- **Owner** - The person or team responsible for developing and delivering the communication. This can be a key leader, communication specialist, project manager, change leader, or designated communication team.

- **Timing** - The schedule or timeline for when the communication will take place. This includes specific dates, and frequency of communication. It ensures that messages are delivered in a timely manner.

- **Reference Materials** - Any supporting materials or resources that will be used in the communication. This can include documents, presentations, videos, infographics, or FAQs that provide additional information and context for stakeholders.

Refer to **Section II** *for* **Toolkit**. Please note that specific details may vary based on the context and requirements of your project or organization.

You can summarize the information of your change in the *Communication Plan* template included in Toolkit Section.

By utilizing this communication plan template and customizing it to your specific change initiative, you can ensure a systematic and strategic approach to stakeholder communication.

Remember, effective communication is the key to engaging stakeholders and building support.

Training, Coaching and Development Plan

As the communication plan lays the foundation for effective engagement and alignment during the change process, it seamlessly leads into the development of the Training, Coaching, and Development Plan. By effectively communicating the change and its associated benefits, you set the stage for stakeholders to understand the importance of acquiring new knowledge and skills.

This natural transition ensures that employees and stakeholders are not only informed about the changes but also provided with the necessary tools and resources to successfully adapt and thrive. With a solid communication strategy in place, the Training, Coaching, and Development Plan builds upon this groundwork, empowering individuals and teams to develop the competencies and capabilities needed to navigate the transformed landscape with confidence and expertise.

"To implement lasting change, we must create an environment conducive to learning."

Some changes are simpler than others. By assessing the skills, knowledge, behaviors, and experiences required for successful change implementation, the Training, Coaching, and Development Plan can identify any potential gaps that may exist.

The plan encompasses various approaches to cater to different development needs:

- **Training:** Provide targeted knowledge and skills for effective role performance, in both face-to-face and online settings

- **Coaching:** Assist individuals or teams in identifying objectives, achieving goals, improving performance, and unlocking potential.

- **Development:** Foster growth and development through mentoring, job rotations, formal education, and alternative learning programs.

The **Change Impact Assessment** describes the impact and affected parties. Additionally, the **Training Assessment** serves as the foundation for developing a comprehensive plan. This will ensure that individuals and teams are equipped with the right information and tools – giving them the confidence to embrace and thrive in a new environment.

Eventually, it will help you identify any skills gaps and informs the development of specific training and development programs to address them. By understanding the existing skills, knowledge, and competencies of individuals and teams, you can determine the areas that require additional support and development.

The **Training Assessment** evaluates the specific training and development needs of employees and stakeholders, ensuring that interventions are targeted, relevant, and impactful. It serves as the foundation for creating a comprehensive plan that provides individuals and teams with the necessary resources to navigate the change process effectively.

Elements of the Training Assessment:

- **Change** - Description of the Change between current state and future state

- **Gap Analysis** - Identify the areas where additional training and development are needed to bridge the gap effectively.

- **Training Needs** - Determine the specific training needs for each stakeholder group. Identify the topics, areas, or competencies where additional training is required.

- **Stakeholder Group** - Stakeholder Group affected by the Change

- **Size of Group** - Approximate number of stakeholders identified with the training need.

- **Training and Development Methods** - Determine the most suitable methods to address the identified needs. This can include a mix of in-person training, e-learning modules, on-the-job training, coaching, mentoring, or workshops.

- **Evaluation Plan** - Outlines the key performance indicators and evaluation methods that will be used to assess the impact of the training on individuals and the organization.

Refer to **Section II** *for* **Toolkit**. Please note that specific details may vary based on the context and requirements of your project or organization.

You can summarize the information of your change in the **Training Assessment** template included in Toolkit Section.

This assessment serves as the basis for designing targeted and impactful training, coaching, and development initiatives that empower individuals and teams to successfully navigate the change and contribute to the organization's overall success.

Now that training needs have been identified, it's time to prepare the Training, Coaching and Development Plan to prepare the stage for training delivery during Step 3: Implementation.

Elements of the Training, Coaching and Development Plan:

- **Topics to be Covered -** An outline of the specific subjects and areas of focus that will be addressed in the training, coaching, and development sessions.

- **Methods of Delivery -** The chosen methods and approaches for delivering the training and coaching sessions, whether it be through workshops, online modules, or one-on-one coaching sessions.

- **Materials to be Used -** The resources and materials that will support the training and coaching initiatives, such as training manuals, online resources, or job aids.

- **Trainers and Coaches -** The skilled professionals who will facilitate the training and coaching sessions, possessing the necessary expertise and experience in the relevant subject matter.

- **Schedule of Sessions -** A detailed schedule outlining the timing and duration of each training and coaching session, allowing participants to plan and prepare accordingly.

*Refer to **Section II** for **Toolkit**.* Please note that specific details may vary based on the context and requirements of your project or organization.

You can summarize the information of your change in the ***Training, Coaching and Development Plan*** template included in Toolkit Section.

By integrating the Training, Coaching, and Development Plan with the Communication Plan, you can ensure that employees are aware of the available training opportunities and are provided with the necessary support to adapt to the changes successfully. This comprehensive approach sets the stage for individuals and teams to acquire the knowledge, skills, and confidence needed to embrace and thrive in the transformed organizational landscape.

Action Plan

With a well-crafted communication plan in place and a thorough understanding of the training and development needs, it is time to transition to the Action Plan as part of the strategy.

The Action Plan serves as the roadmap for successfully implementing the change according to defined timelines, milestones, and assigned responsibilities. It integrates the activities required to execute the change into the project plan, ensuring that all aspects of the initiative are covered. By creating a comprehensive action plan, you can establish clear expectations, allocate necessary resources, and define monitoring and evaluation metrics. Effective leadership, combined with a well-defined strategy and a capable team, will be essential in navigating any challenges that may arise.

Integrating change management and project management plans occurs during this phase.

Based on the assessment of the change's impact, the Action Plan outlines the steps, resources, and key milestones necessary for a successful implementation. It identifies the timeline, action items, assigned responsibilities, and required resources to effectively execute the change. The plan ensures that everyone involved understands their roles and responsibilities, and that they have the necessary resources and support to execute their tasks.

It's important to make sure that everyone involved understands their roles and responsibilities, and that they have the necessary resources and support to execute their tasks.

Elements of the Action Plan:

- **Action Item** - Specific tasks or activities that need to be completed to achieve the objectives of the change initiative. Each action item should be clearly defined and measurable to ensure accountability and progress tracking.

- **Responsible** - Individual or team assigned to carry out the action item. They are responsible for completing the task within the specified timeframe and ensuring its successful execution.

- **References** - Any supporting documents, resources, or materials that are relevant to the action item. These references provide additional information, guidelines, or instructions that can aid in completing the task effectively.

- **Start Date** - When the action item is scheduled to begin. It serves as a reference point for tracking progress and ensuring that tasks are initiated at the appropriate time.

- **End Date** - Deadline or target date for completing the action item. It provides a clear timeframe for accomplishing the task and helps in monitoring progress and adherence to timelines.

- **Status** - Progress and current state of completion. It can be categorized as "In progress," "Completed," "Pending," or any other relevant status that indicates the stage of the task.

Refer to **Section II** *for* **Toolkit**. Please note that specific details may vary based on the context and requirements of your project or organization.

You can summarize the information of your change in the *Action Plan* template included in Toolkit Section.

The elements of the action plan work together to provide structure, accountability, and transparency in executing the necessary tasks for implementing the change initiative. By clearly defining action items, assigning responsibilities, providing references, establishing start and end dates, and tracking the status of each task, organizations can ensure that the necessary actions are taken to drive successful change implementation.

The plan should be communicated to all stakeholders, including employees, customers, and any other parties that may be affected by the change. This includes providing regular updates on the change and its progress, as well as addressing any concerns or questions that stakeholders may have.

Managing Risks

An important aspect of the Action Plan is to identify and manage any risks or issues that may arise during the change process. This proactive approach helps anticipate potential challenges and provides strategies for addressing them effectively. By addressing risks and issues in a timely manner, you can minimize disruptions and keep the change implementation on track.

- **Risk Monitoring and Evaluation:** Continuously monitor and evaluate identified risks throughout the change process. This involves tracking the effectiveness of risk mitigation strategies, identifying new risks that may emerge, and making adjustments to the mitigation plan as necessary.

- **Communication and Reporting:** Keep stakeholders informed about identified risks, mitigation strategies, and the progress of risk management efforts. Regular reporting and updates on risk status help maintain transparency and ensure stakeholders' confidence in the change initiative.

Elements of the Risk Mitigation Plan:

- **Risk Identification:** Identify potential risks that may affect the change initiative. It is important to consider both internal and external factors that could impact the project, such as resource constraints, technology limitations, stakeholder resistance, or regulatory changes.

- **Risk Mitigation Strategies:** Develop specific actions or strategies to minimize or eliminate identified risks. Mitigation strategies may include developing contingency plans, conducting additional training or education, implementing communication plans, or adjusting project timelines and resources.

- **Risk Ownership and Accountability:** Assign ownership and accountability for managing risks. Each identified risk should have a responsible individual or team tasked with monitoring, implementing mitigation strategies, and reporting on the progress of risk management efforts.

Refer to **Section II** *for* **Toolkit.** Please note that specific details may vary based on the context and requirements of your project or organization.

You can summarize the information of your change in the *Risk Mitigation Plan* template included in Toolkit Section.

By incorporating a comprehensive Risk Mitigation Plan into the Action Plan, you can proactively manage risks, anticipate potential challenges, and respond effectively to unforeseen circumstances. This helps to ensure the successful implementation of the change initiative while minimizing disruptions and maximizing positive outcomes.

Metrics and Tracking Tools

In addition to defining the activities and responsibilities, the Action Plan should also include metrics and tracking tools to monitor and evaluate the progress and results of the change implementation. This helps you measure the effectiveness of the change efforts and make any necessary adjustments along the way. By tracking metrics and using appropriate tracking tools, you can ensure that the change is progressing as planned and identify areas where additional support or modifications may be needed.

By implementing a well-defined **Action Plan**, you can effectively integrate the change initiative into the overall **Project Plan**, ensuring alignment, coordination, and successful outcomes.

Rewards and Recognition

Recognizing and rewarding progress and achievements are important elements of the Strategy. Establishing rewards and recognition systems motivates and reinforces positive behaviors and outcomes, driving continued commitment and engagement from stakeholders. By celebrating achievements and milestones throughout the change process, organizations create a positive and supportive environment that encourages and sustains momentum.

From Strategy to Action...

With the strategy in place, it's time to act. This transition marks the start of implementing the strategy and taking the necessary steps to drive change within the organization. The next steps focus on implementing new processes, monitoring performance, and continuously improving to ensure ongoing success. It's the moment when the strategy comes alive, and the organization embarks on a transformative journey towards its goals.

Develop the Strategy

STEP 2

THINGS TO REMEMBER:

- Review business processes and identify the changes.

- Define clear metrics and targets by establishing appropriate and relevant key performance indicators (KPI).

- Assess the impact of the change on people, process, technology, and resources.

- Identify and analyze stakeholders affected by the change.

- Develop a comprehensive communication plan.

- Identify training needs and plan accordingly.

- Create an action plan. Review regularly.

- Acknowledge and reward desired behaviors for modeling.

- Celebrate successes to motivate stakehodlers.

Going Paperless: Electronic Batch Record Project

During the strategy phase of the Electronic Batch Record (EBR) project, we focused on developing a comprehensive strategy to streamline and digitize batch record management. A thorough process review was performed, identifying inefficiencies and opportunities for automation throughout the workflow. Additionally, an impact assessment was conducted to evaluate the opportunities, risks, and potential challenges associated with the transition to a paperless process. It considered different aspects of the organization, such as operational workflows, employee roles and responsibilities, data management processes, and regulatory compliance requirements.

Stakeholder analysis and engagement were prioritized during this phase. The team assessed the individuals and groups affected by the EBR implementation to tailor communication and engagement strategies. Regular updates and notifications were shared to keep stakeholders informed and involved.

The technology infrastructure, including data migration, was carefully addressed. The team evaluated the existing infrastructure, identified requirements for implementing the EBR system, and coordinated the setup and configuration to ensure a seamless integration.

Change management and training were key considerations. A change management plan was developed to address potential resistance and facilitate a cultural shift towards the paperless process. A comprehensive training program was designed to ensure employee proficiency in the use of computers, new system, including classroom and online sessions and one-on-one coaching.

A well-defined communication strategy was established, recognizing its importance in gaining support and maintaining stakeholder engagement. Various channels, such as email updates, town hall meetings, and dedicated training sessions, were utilized to deliver consistent and timely communication.

Risk assessment and mitigation were integrated into the strategy phase. We conducted thorough analyses to identify potential obstacles and developed strategies to proactively manage risks. Regular reviews were conducted to maintain effective risk management.

By carefully planning and executing these activities, we laid a solid foundation for the successful implementation of the EBR system. The strategy phase not only set the project's direction but also ensured the necessary resources were in place and prepared the organization for the transition to a paperless batch record management system.

Having completed the strategy phase, we were prepared to move forward with the implementation of the EBR system. Through a comprehensive strategy development process, the team was fully equipped to bring the vision of a paperless batch record management system to reality.

Step 3
Implement

**"Effective implementation requires
both discipline and consistency,
as it is the bridge that connects
ideas to actual results."**

Once you and your team have completed defining the strategy and setting the plans, it is time to move into the implementation phase. This is where ideas begin to take shape and change is brought to life. In this step, you need to stay focused on the end goal while paying close attention to the details. Implementing change requires effective execution of the plans developed during the earlier stages.

In this step, you will find how to execute your implementation plans, communicate with stakeholders, provide training and skill development, reinforce new business routines, and monitor progress to ensure a successful implementation.

Making the Change Work

To successfully implement the change, you need to deploy the necessary resources. This includes allocating human resources, leveraging appropriate technology, securing adequate financial investments, and obtaining any other required assets. By ensuring that the right resources are in place, you can carry out the necessary activities and tasks effectively.

Throughout the implementation phase, **monitoring progress** and **tracking key metrics** play a vital role. This allows you to measure the success of the implementation and adjust as necessary. By regularly assessing the progress and performance against established metrics, you can gauge the effectiveness of the changes and identify areas that may require additional attention or modifications.

Regular reviews and adjustments are essential for successful implementation because the plan of action is not set in stone. They should be flexible enough to accommodate new insights and challenges that may arise. By conducting periodic reviews, your team can identify potential issues, assess the progress made, and make necessary adjustments to ensure that the implementation stays on track and aligns with your overall goals and objectives.

"Continuous evaluations and adaptive modifications fuel the engine of change, driving it towards accomplishment."

Additionally, you must constantly explore and consider **risk mitigation strategies**. By conducting a thorough risk assessment and developing mitigation plans, you can proactively identify and address potential obstacles. This includes establishing contingency plans, maintaining open communication channels, and regularly reassessing risks throughout the implementation process. Doing these will help you enhance the chances of a smooth and successful implementation while minimizing the impact of unforeseen risks.

Regular progress updates and metrics tracking provide valuable insights into the effectiveness of the implemented changes. By monitoring and analyzing key metrics, you can assess the impact of the changes and identify any areas that require further focus or improvement. This information enables you to make informed decisions and take corrective actions when necessary to ensure the success of the implementation.

This phase is also an opportunity to showcase the positive impact of the changes and generate excitement among stakeholders. By focusing on **quick wins and tangible**

results, you can lay a strong foundation for the successful implementation of the desired changes. By identifying specific areas where improvements can be realized quickly, you can showcase the immediate advantages of the changes. These quick wins can be achieved by streamlining processes, eliminating redundancies, or improving efficiency in targeted areas. By highlighting the positive outcomes early on, you can generate buy-in from stakeholders and create a sense of momentum and progress.

Reviewing Procedures and Approvals

Depending on the type of changes, there can be projects that require a lot of changes in procedures. This can be a critical activity during the implementation phase. It is important to review existing procedures and make necessary updates as necessary, based on the process reviews conducted. This ensures that procedures align with the new changes and support the successful implementation.

Existing procedures should be reviewed to identify any misalignments with the proposed changes. This involves assessing the effectiveness and efficiency of current procedures and determining whether modifications are required. Redlining or creating new procedures may be necessary to reflect the updated processes.

When reviewing procedures, make sure to identify areas that need improvement or modification. Redlining, which involves marking up existing procedures to indicate changes, can help highlight necessary revisions. Additionally, new procedures may need to be created to document processes that were not previously in place.

Once the procedures have been reviewed and updated, an **approval process** should be established to ensure that all changes are authorized and documented. This may involve obtaining approvals from relevant stakeholders, such as department heads or subject matter experts. Clear communication and documentation of the approval process are essential for maintaining accountability and ensuring that the revised procedures are officially recognized.

Timing is critical in procedures, revisions and approvals. To complete the reviewing procedures and approvals efficiently, consider the following suggestions:

- **Establish a Procedure Review Team:** Form a dedicated team responsible for conducting the procedure reviews, redlining, and creating new procedures. This team should include subject matter experts and representatives from relevant departments to ensure comprehensive and accurate reports.

- **Set Clear Deadlines:** Set limits and timelines for each stage of the procedure review process. This helps create a sense of urgency and accountability, ensuring that the reviews and approvals are completed in a timely manner.

- **Utilize Collaboration Tools:** Implement digital collaboration tools that facilitate real-time collaboration and document sharing. This allows team members to work together efficiently, track changes, and streamline the approval process.

- **Communicate and Seek Feedback:** Maintain communication channels with stakeholders involved in the procedure review and approval process. Regularly update them on progress, seek their input and feedback, and address any concerns or questions promptly.

- **Streamline Approval Workflow:** Design an efficient approval workflow that clearly outlines the steps, roles, and responsibilities involved in the approval process. This ensures that approvals are obtained in a systematic and timely manner, reducing potential bottlenecks.

- **Document and Archive:** Secure proper documentation of all reviewed and approved procedures. Establish a centralized repository or document management system to store the revised procedures for easy access and future reference.

By following these suggestions and implementing an organized and efficient approach, you can effectively review procedures, make necessary updates, obtain approvals, and ensure that the revised procedures are implemented in a timely manner to support the overall implementation process.

Communication and Stakeholder Engagement

Effective communication is key to successful implementation. This is your opportunity to establish clear and consistent messaging to effectively communicate the purpose, goals, and benefits of the change to all stakeholders. Building upon the previously completed Communication Plan, you will craft concise and relevant messages to create a shared understanding of the change and generate stakeholder buy-in. Regular updates and progress reports, as outlined in the Communication Plan, will maintain transparency, build trust, and sustain stakeholder engagement. By delivering updates through various channels, stakeholders feel involved, valued, and empowered to give feedback.

Communication Strategies for Stakeholder Engagement:

In addition to tailoring communication strategies based on stakeholders' levels of impact and influence, there are general communication strategies that can further enhance stakeholder engagement and support. These strategies are applicable across various stakeholder groups and can strengthen overall communication effectiveness.

By incorporating these general strategies alongside the targeted approaches, you can create a comprehensive communication plan that addresses the diverse needs, concerns, and perspectives of stakeholders. The following communication strategies should be considered:

- **Build a Compelling Case:** Clearly state reasons for the change, emphasizing benefits and positive outcomes. Provide evidence and address concerns to build trust.

- **Tailor Messages to Stakeholder Needs:** Customize communication to address specific interests and priorities. Emphasize alignment with goals and values.

- **Show Empathy and Understanding:** Acknowledge challenges and offer support for stakeholders. Actively listen, answer questions, and make them feel safe.

- **Foster Two-Way Communication:** Encourage stakeholder input, suggestions, and feedback. Seek opinions and include ideas in decision-making processes.

- **Provide Timely and Transparent Updates:** Keep stakeholders informed with regular updates. Share successes, milestones, and adjustments transparently.

- **Engage Key Influencers:** Identify influential stakeholders as advocates for the change. Seek their support in promoting benefits to their respective groups.

- **Offer Training and Resources:** Equip stakeholders with necessary training, resources, and support for successful change adaptation.

- **Recognize and Celebrate Progress:** Publicly acknowledge milestones and stakeholders' contributions to implementing the change.

- **Establish a Feedback Mechanism:** Encourage ongoing stakeholder feedback, actively listening and taking appropriate action.

- **Continuously Evaluate and Improve:** Regularly assess communication strategies, seeking stakeholder feedback for refinement and enhancement.

Addressing Stakeholder Concerns and Questions

During the implementation phase, stakeholders may have concerns or questions about the change. This is normal and it indicates their engagement and interest. Addressing these is the backbone of effective communication. It creates a supportive environment where stakeholders feel comfortable expressing their concerns and seeking clarification. Utilize the communication channels and platforms specified in the Communication Plan, such as **hosting Q&A sessions** or providing a **dedicated communication channel or medium,** to give stakeholders a platform to voice their concerns and receive transparent and honest responses.

Managing changes effectively requires active listening and empathetic communication. Your team should be responsive and provide clear explanations to alleviate anxieties and misconceptions. By openly addressing concerns, trust can be built, resistance can be mitigated, and stakeholder confidence in the change can be increased. Regularly scheduled forums, such as **town hall meetings, Q&A sessions, or dedicated communication channels,** provide opportunities for stakeholders to voice their concerns and ask questions. Document and address these concerns promptly, providing transparent and honest responses that demonstrate a commitment to stakeholder engagement and satisfaction.

By incorporating these strategies and addressing stakeholder concerns and questions, you can foster effective communication, build trust, and ensure stakeholder engagement throughout the implementation process.

Training and Development

Another key aspect to ensure a successful implementation is prioritizing training and skill development for personnel. By providing customized training programs tailored to individual roles and skill levels, employees can acquire the necessary competencies to navigate the changes effectively.

As the change is implemented, personnel may require new skills or knowledge to adapt successfully. Based on the outcomes of the training needs assessment and the training, coaching, and development plan conducted in Step 2, you need to develop customized **training programs.** Aligning **the training content and delivery methods** with the identified needs enables employees to gain the competencies to perform their new responsibilities with confidence.

"Investing in training and development drives organizational growth during implementation."

Building on the training needs assessment performed, customized training programs can be developed to address specific knowledge gaps.

If the assessment identified a **knowledge gap** in customer service skills, the program may include modules on active listening, effective communication, and problem-solving techniques tailored to the specific roles and responsibilities of the personnel involved.

Recognizing that individuals have varying levels of expertise and responsibilities, training programs should be tailored to address **role-specific requirements** and skill gaps. Referring to the training, coaching, and development plan, the training should be designed to bridge any identified gaps in skills and competencies.

⇒In a system implementation project, the training program can be tailored to different user groups based on their roles and responsibilities with managers focusing on system administration and reporting, while front-line employees concentrate on using the system for daily tasks and customer interactions.

To accommodate diverse learning preferences and accessibility needs, training should be delivered through a variety of formats, such as **classroom training sessions, on-the-job mentoring, virtual learning platforms, or e-learning modules.** By offering multiple training formats, the team can cater to different learning styles and maximize knowledge transfer.

⇒In a change initiative, a blended approach to training can be implemented combining interactive classroom sessions, on-the-job mentoring for practical application and self-paced e-learning modules for remote access.

By prioritizing training and skill development, organizations can equip their personnel with the necessary knowledge and capabilities to adapt successfully to the changes. Customized training programs, tailored to individual roles and skill levels, and delivered through various formats, ensure that employees receive the support they need to thrive during the implementation process. Drawing on the outcomes of the training needs assessment and the training, coaching, and development plan, organizations can design and deliver effective training programs that empower employees and drive the success of the implementation.

Reinforcing New Business Routines

To ensure the changes are embedded effectively, you must establish accountability mechanisms and reinforce new business routines. This involves implementing the following strategies:

Defining Clear Roles and Responsibilities

To reinforce the new routines, it is essential to clearly define the roles and responsibilities of employees involved in the implementation process. This helps create clarity and accountability, ensuring that everyone understands their specific contributions to the new routines. By establishing clear roles and responsibilities, employees can take ownership of their tasks and actively participate in the implementation.

> ⇒ In a process improvement initiative, different team members may be assigned specific responsibilities for implementing and monitoring the new processes. This can include individuals responsible for data entry, quality control, or processing documentation. By assigning clear roles and responsibilities, each team member understands their specific contributions to the new routines.

Setting Up Performance Metrics

In the previous step, you identified the performance metrics and targets for the change initiative. Now, in this step, these metrics come into play. They serve as benchmarks to track progress and measure the effectiveness of the changes.

> ⇒ In a customer service improvement initiative, metrics like average response time and customer satisfaction ratings help assess the impact of new routines.

By consistently monitoring these metrics, you can identify areas for improvement and make data-driven decisions.

Performance metrics ensure alignment with strategic objectives and drive continuous improvement throughout the implementation process.

Ongoing Coaching and Support

To support employees in navigating the new business routines, ongoing coaching and support should be provided. This can include providing guidance, answering questions, and offering resources to help employees adapt to the changes. By offering continuous support, employees feel empowered and confident in their abilities to perform the new routines effectively.

⇒ In a software implementation project, dedicated training sessions can be conducted to help employees become familiar with the new software and workflows. Additionally, subject matter experts or mentors can be assigned to provide ongoing coaching and support, addressing any challenges or concerns that arise during the transition period.

Regular Check-ins and Progress Meetings

Open channels of communication are essential to reinforce the new business routines. Regular meetings provide an opportunity to review progress, address any issues or roadblocks, and make necessary adjustments as needed. By consistently monitoring the implementation progress, you can ensure that the new routines are being followed and identify any areas that require additional support or improvement.

⇒ Weekly or monthly team meetings can be scheduled to discuss the implementation progress, share best practices, and address any challenges encountered. These meetings create a forum for employees to provide updates, seek guidance, and collaborate on finding solutions to overcome obstacles.

By reinforcing new business routines, you can ensure the sustainability of the changes over time. By defining clear roles and responsibilities, setting up performance metrics, providing ongoing coaching and support, and conducting regular check-ins, employees are empowered to embrace them and drive the desired outcomes of the implementation. This commitment to reinforcing business routines creates a lasting impact and sets the foundation for continuous improvement and growth.

Monitoring and Adjustment

To ensure the success of the implementation, you need to continuously monitor progress and make necessary adjustments. By regularly reviewing project timelines and go-live dates, you can stay on track and ensure timely completion of the implementation. Additionally, analyzing metrics and gathering feedback provides valuable insights into the effectiveness of the implemented changes and helps identify areas for improvement. By actively monitoring and adjusting, you can ensure that the implementation stays aligned with the overall objectives and goals.

Tracking Tools

- Documentation
- Training
- Communications
- Action Plan
- Risks

Tracking Tools:

To facilitate monitoring and adjustment, the following tracking tools are essential:

⇒ **Documentation:** Maintain records of project plans, progress reports, and any relevant documentation to track the implementation process.

⇒ **Training:** Keep track of training activities, attendance, and assessments to ensure employees receive the necessary development and support.

⇒ **Communications:** Document communication efforts, including key messages, channels used, and stakeholder responses, to evaluate the effectiveness of communication strategies.

⇒ **Action Plan:** Track the progress of action items identified in the action plan to ensure timely completion and alignment with the implementation goals.

⇒ **Risks:** Continuously assess and monitor identified risks, updating risk mitigation plans as needed to minimize potential obstacles.

To maintain progress and stay on track, **regularly review project timelines and go-live dates.** This allows you to assess the status of the implementation, identify any delays or bottlenecks, and take appropriate actions to address them.

⇒ Conduct **weekly or monthly reviews** of the project timeline to track the progress of key activities and deliverables.

⇒ Identify any tasks that are behind schedule and take **necessary measures to mitigate** the delays, such as reallocating resources or adjusting priorities.

Metrics and feedback provide valuable insights into the effectiveness of the implemented changes and help identify areas for improvement. Regularly analyze relevant metrics to assess the impact of the changes on key performance indicators and desired outcomes. Additionally, gather feedback from stakeholders, employees, and customers to gain a holistic understanding of their experiences and perceptions of the changes.

⇒ Utilize **surveys, interviews, and focus groups** to collect feedback from stakeholders and employees.

⇒ Analyze **quantitative and qualitative data** to evaluate the success of the implementation and identify opportunities for refinement. Consider **metrics** such as customer satisfaction ratings, employee productivity levels, or process efficiency metrics.

Based on the insights gained from reviewing metrics and gathering feedback, make necessary adjustments to the implementation. This may involve modifying processes, reallocating resources, or refining the communication and training strategies. Be responsive and adaptive, addressing any issues or challenges that arise to ensure that the implementation aligns with the desired outcomes.

- If the analysis of metrics reveals a decline in customer satisfaction, revisit customer service processes and make improvements.

⇒ If feedback from employees indicates a need for additional training or support, adjust to enhance their capabilities and confidence in executing the new routines.

By actively monitoring the implementation progress and making necessary adjustments, you can optimize the effectiveness of the change initiative. This ongoing monitoring and adjustment process ensures that the implementation remains aligned with the overall objectives and goals, increasing the likelihood of achieving the desired outcomes. In the next step, Step 4: Achieve Results, we will focus on evaluating the outcomes of the change initiative and celebrating successes along the way.

Successful implementation goes beyond executing the change; it involves continuously monitoring results, analyzing data, and making adjustments to drive continuous improvement and enhance the overall impact of the change.

Implement

- Implement your plan and track metrics.

- Measure progress and adjust as needed.

- Look for quick wins to build momentum.

- Communicate messages clearly and consistently.

- Provide training for your people as needed to help them adapt to changes and innovation.

- Reinforce new business routines to sustain best practices.

- Ensure tasks are completed on time.

- Track the progress.

- Make thorough documentation of all changes and progress.

- Continuously measure progress using relevant metrics to ensure you stay on course and updated.

Going Paperless: Electronic Batch Record Project

Significant progress and achievements were made during the Step 3: Implementation Phase of the Electronic Batch Record (EBR) project. It was a long process, since multiple areas were impacted. The team successfully set up the necessary infrastructure, conducted meticulous data migration, and focused on quick wins to demonstrate the immediate benefits of the paperless process.

Manual processes were automated, eliminating duplication of data entry, and improving inventory management efficiency. These initiatives showcased the immediate advantages of going paperless and increased enthusiasm among stakeholders.

Employee training and effective communication played vital roles in ensuring a smooth transition. Comprehensive train ing sessions were conducted. Job aids and user manuals were created to serve as references and support employees in navigating the new digital processes. The team also provided one -on-one coaching to address individual needs.

Effective communication was paramount throughout the project. We consistently communicated project updates, milestones, and changes to all stakeholders, including employees, suppliers, and customers. Various communication channels were utilized, such as email updates, town hall meetings, and dedicated training sessions, to keep everyone informed and engaged. We also organized a two-day hands-on event that showcased the new technology, featuring a popular movie series!

Throughout the implementation, unexpected events inevitably occurred, but the team remained fully committed and adaptable. We made the necessary adjustments to keep the project on track. With the accomplishments in mind, we were ready to move into **Step 4: Achieve Results**, where we evaluate the outcomes of the EBR implementation and celebrate the successes along the way.

Step 4
Achieve Results

"Results reflect our choices and actions. Stay focused on your goals."

After successfully implementing the change initiative in Step 3, it is now time to focus on achieving the desired results. You will see how it involves evaluating the performance and outcomes of the change effort and setting performance metrics and targets. These will help you assess the impact of the change, recognize achievements, and ensure that everything is aligned with your goals. Eventually, if you are consistent, it will surely bring about lasting benefits and sustained growth.

As you begin shifting your efforts toward evaluation, it will be necessary to establish a structured framework to help you better monitor and track your progress. The succeeding parts in this step will assist you in making this happen.

Evaluating Performance and Outcomes

The outcome evaluation provides an opportunity to assess the overall success of the implementation and understand the extent to which the predefined goals and objectives have been met. By analyzing the results, you can identify strengths and weaknesses, and make necessary adjustments to enhance the desired outcomes. This evaluation process enables you to examine the data and insights obtained, leading to a better understanding of the effectiveness of the change initiative.

⇒ A customer service improvement initiative aimed to reduce complaint resolution time by 30%. The evaluation revealed a 25% reduction, indicating success with room for improvement. Additional training for customer service representatives in handling complex complaints was identified to bridge the gap and achieve the desired outcome.

⇒ A new software system implementation aimed to improve data accuracy by reducing error rates. The evaluation showed a significant reduction in errors, surpassing the target. Stakeholder feedback highlighted the need for user interface enhancements to enhance the overall user experience and maximize the benefits of the system.

Analyze Data and Results: Evaluate the collected data and performance metrics to identify areas for improvement and optimization. Look for patterns and trends that require attention. Assess established KPIs to measure actual performance against predefined indicators, gaining insights into the success of the change initiative. Analyze relevant data, both quantitative and qualitative, to identify areas for improvement and develop action plans.

⇒ Analyze customer satisfaction scores, process cycle times, and employee productivity to reveal specific areas for enhancements such as reducing response times or streamlining workflows.

Making Data-Driven Decisions: Use the evaluation findings and insights to make data-driven decisions. Based on the results and feedback, determine whether any adjustments or interventions are necessary to optimize the change initiative. This may involve revisiting action plans, refining processes, or reallocating resources to ensure continuous progress toward the desired results.

⇒ Using customer feedback data to identify areas for improvement in the service delivery process and implementing changes to address customer concerns.

It is good to remember that evaluating performance and outcomes is more than just a formality, a requirement, or a box to be ticked off. It is an ongoing process that demands attention, analysis, and commitment. When you actively engage your team in this process, you will sustain the successful change effort you began and improve on the areas that need fine-tuning.

Communicating Results

Communicating the results helps reinforce the positive impact of the change initiative, celebrate successes, and maintain transparency throughout the organization. It is an opportunity to recognize the efforts of individuals and teams involved, foster a culture of continuous improvement, and motivate stakeholders to embrace future changes.

Clear Messaging: Craft a clear and concise message that highlights the key outcomes and achievements of the initiative. Use language that is easily understandable by all stakeholders. Ensure that the message is transparent, providing a balanced view of both successes and areas for improvement.

Tailored Communication Channels: Select appropriate communication channels to reach different stakeholders effectively. This could include town hall meetings, team meetings, email updates, newsletters, intranet platforms, or project dashboards. Consider the preferences and needs of various stakeholders to ensure the message reaches them in a timely and accessible manner.

Engage Stakeholders: Encourage stakeholders to ask questions and provide feedback regarding the results and outcomes of the initiative. Create a supportive environment where stakeholders feel comfortable sharing their thoughts, concerns, and suggestions.

Address Areas for Improvements: Acknowledge and address areas for improvement identified through the evaluation process. Communicate the organization's commitment to ongoing improvement and its plans to address the identified gaps.

Transparent and tailored communication helps build trust, encourages stakeholder buy-in, and fosters a culture of continuous improvement and growth within the organization.

Celebrating Successes and Recognizing Achievements

To reinforce the positive impact of the change and encourage continued engagement and motivation, you may want to celebrate success and recognize achievements! It will not only acknowledge the efforts and contributions of individuals and teams involved in the change, but it will surely create a sense of accomplishment and motivation within the organization.

"Success drives the journey. Celebrate milestones, recognize contributions, and inspire continuous growth."

Here are some key points to consider when celebrating successes and recognizing achievements:

Acknowledge Milestones: Identify and acknowledge significant milestones that have been achieved throughout the change initiative. This could include reaching key targets, completing major project phases, or successfully implementing new processes or systems. Recognizing these milestones highlights progress and builds momentum for further success.

⇒ Celebrating the successful completion of a complex system implementation project by hosting a recognition event where team members are acknowledged for their hard work and dedication.

Recognize Individuals and Teams: Appreciate and build on the efforts of individuals and teams who have contributed to the success of the change initiative. This can be done through formal recognition programs, team meetings, or personalized appreciation messages. Acknowledging their contributions boosts morale, fosters a sense of pride, and encourages continued dedication.

⇒ Sending personalized thank-you notes to team members who played a significant role in achieving a specific project milestone, highlighting their specific contributions and the positive impact they made.

Share Success Stories: Highlight the positive outcomes and benefits resulting from the change. Tell stories that inspire and motivate others by demonstrating the value and significance of the change initiative. Emphasize the challenges overcome, lessons learned, and the positive impact on individuals, teams, and the organization as a whole.

⇒ Creating a case study or success story document that showcases the transformational impact of the change initiative, including testimonials from stakeholders who have experienced the benefits firsthand.

Align Recognition with Organizational Values: Ensure that the recognition and celebration align with the organization's values and desired culture. Recognize behaviors and achievements that exemplify the organization's core values and reinforce the desired norms and behaviors associated with the change initiative.

⇒ Recognizing those who have demonstrated exceptional collaboration, innovation, or adaptability in driving the change initiative forward, highlighting how their actions align with the organization's values.

By celebrating successes and recognizing achievements, you reinforce the positive impact of the change, boost morale, and inspire continued engagement and dedication. It creates a sense of pride and accomplishment among individuals and teams, fostering a culture of continuous improvement and driving ongoing success.

With the achievements celebrated and the outcomes evaluated in Step 4, organizations gain valuable insights and a solid foundation for the next phase: Step 5, Improve and Grow. This phase focuses on continuous improvement and leveraging the momentum gained from the successful change initiative to drive further enhancements and growth. By building upon the lessons learned, optimizing processes, and embracing a culture of continuous improvement, organizations can unlock their full potential and achieve sustainable growth and success.

Achieve Results

STEP 4 — THINGS TO REMEMBER:

- Compare results against predefined goals and objectives.

- Measure and compare actual performance against predefined indicators.

- Engage with stakeholders to gather feedback on satisfaction, perceptions, and suggestions for improvements.

- Use data to identify areas for improvement and decision-making.

- Recognize and appreciate efforts.

- Celebrate successes.

- Maintain documentation of processes, strategies, and outcomes.

- Create knowledge transfer materials and resources for future learning.

- Revisit areas that needs improvement and resolutely address them.

Going Paperless: Electronic Batch Record Project

Going back to our project, once the system went live, during Step 4: Achieve Results, we established a 24x7 support system. We understood that change could be daunting, especially when transitioning from familiar paper-based processes to a digital system. By offering round-the-clock support, we aimed to provide reassurance and guidance whenever it was needed. This commitment to support fostered a sense of confidence and empowerment among the manufacturing personnel, allowing them to embrace the change with greater ease and enthusiasm.

Another key area of attention was the collection and analysis of cycle time data. The team diligently monitored the time taken to complete various manufacturing processes, aiming to identify areas for improvement and track our progress. Additionally, the team actively sought feedback from operators and other end users involved in the manufacturing processes.

We recognized the importance of their perspectives and experiences in shaping the success of the EBR system. Having open and transparent communication channels, we gathered feedback that allowed us to address any concerns, provide necessary support, and make iterative improvements to the system and associated processes. This ensured that the implementation was truly aligned with the needs and expectations of the people on the manufacturing floor.

Data analysis played a crucial role in the achievement of our desired outcomes. We analyzed the collected data, seeking patterns, trends, and opportunities for improvement. The impact of the new system was measure on cycle time reduction and overall efficiency gains. Results were reported to management and all relevant stakeholders, highlighting the progress made and the positive impact of the EBR system. We ensured transparency and kept everyone informed and engaged throughout the project.

The evaluation of metrics within the weigh dispensing and manufacturing areas revealed the exceptional commitment and engagement of our end users. They were fully aware of the benefits the new system and processes brought to their work, and their active participation played a significant role in the successful implementation. Their willingness to embrace change, adapt to new ways of working, and actively contribute to the continuous improvement efforts showcased their dedication and passion for driving positive transformations within our organization.

Recognizing the remarkable efforts, commitment, and leadership shown by our team members, we made it a point to acknowledge and celebrate their contributions. We publicly acknowledged and appreciated the dedication, teamwork, and initiative demonstrated by them throughout the project. This recognition not only boosted morale but also reinforced the collaborative and supportive culture we aimed to foster within the organization.

The recognition and celebration of our team's efforts during the project served as a testament to their commitment, teamwork, and leadership skills. As we concluded Step 4, we were filled with a sense of accomplishment and readiness for the next phase of our journey. The achievements and lessons learned during this step prepared the team for the future. Let's dive in to **Step 5: Improve and Grow.**

Step 5
Improve and Grow

"Continuous improvement is the key to unlocking your full potential."

To sustain and build upon your achievements, you must improve continuously. This step will cover how managing changes effectively will keep you growing. By encouraging employee involvement, identifying improvement opportunities, and promoting ongoing growth and innovation, you can continuously enhance their performance and drive long-term success.

Sustaining the Change

To ensure that your change initiative succeeds, you need to adopt a holistic and innovative approach to your organizational culture and routines. This includes identifying areas that require ongoing support, additional resources, or further training. This will help you develop the right strategies to implement regular performance reviews and ongoing communication, which will ensure that the achieved results are maintained over the long term.

Gathering Stakeholder Feedback: Engage with stakeholders to gather their perspectives and feedback on the implemented changes. This can be done through surveys, interviews, focus groups, or other feedback mechanisms. By understanding stakeholder perceptions and experiences, organizations can identify areas for improvement and optimize the change initiative. For example,

⇒ Conducting post-implementation surveys can provide valuable insights into stakeholder satisfaction and suggestions for improvement.

Documentation and Knowledge Transfer: To facilitate continuous improvement and knowledge sharing, it is important to document the entire implementation process, including the strategies, actions, and outcomes. This ensures that valuable insights and information are preserved for future reference.

⇒ Create knowledge transfer materials and resources such as comprehensive project reports, best practice guides, or training materials can be shared with relevant stakeholders, future teams, or other departments within the organization. This enables the organization to benefit from the lessons learned and avoid reinventing the wheel in future initiatives.

Sustainability and Maintenance: Develop strategies to ensure ongoing support, updates, and improvements to maintain the desired outcomes and maximize the return on investment.

⇒ Establish mechanisms for regular maintenance activities, conducting periodic reviews, and implement feedback loops to help identify areas that require adjustments or enhancements to maintain the desired outcomes.

"Foster a culture of continuous improvement, where innovation and growth are valued, by celebrating successes, reflecting on experiences, and sharing lessons learned."

Continuous Improvement and Optimization

Use the celebration of successes and achievements as an opportunity to emphasize the importance of continuous improvement and learning. Encourage individuals and teams to reflect on their experiences, share lessons learned, and identify areas for further enhancement. By fostering a culture of continuous improvement, you create an environment where innovation and growth are valued.

Lessons Learned and Future Improvements: Reflect on the lessons learned from the change initiative and apply them to future improvement efforts. Capture and document key insights, successes, challenges, and best practices that emerged during the implementation. These lessons learned serve as a valuable resource for identifying areas of optimization and avoiding pitfalls in future initiatives.

⇒ Conduct a lesson-learned workshop or review session to gather input from project team members and stakeholders, discussing what worked well, what could have been improved, and identifying actionable recommendations for future improvements.

Implement Changes and Enhancements: Based on the feedback received, data analysis, and lessons learned, implement changes and enhancements to further optimize the processes, systems, or strategies that were part of the change initiative. These changes can range from minor adjustments to major process redesigns, depending on the identified areas of improvement.

⇒ Updating standard operating procedures based on feedback and lessons learned to streamline and simplify processes, incorporating automation or technology to improve efficiency and accuracy.

Foster a Culture of Innovation and Agility: Encourage a culture of continuous improvement and innovation within the organization. Create channels for employees to contribute ideas and suggestions for improvement and provide support and resources to implement those ideas. Emphasize the importance of agility and adaptability in responding to changing market dynamics and customer needs.

⇒ Establishing an employee suggestion program or innovation challenge to encourage employees to propose and implement ideas for process improvements or new ways of working.

Embracing continuous improvement fuels organizational evolution, ensuring lasting alignment with goals. Through feedback, analysis, lessons learned, and implementation, success endures, adaptability thrives, and performance excels. Cultivating innovation, agility, and relentless learning empowers organizations to flourish amidst dynamic landscapes.

Continuous Improvement Culture

When you cultivate a mindset of innovation, you will promote a culture of continuous improvement and growth.

Leveraging Expertise and Building Confidence:

Successful change implementation brings **valuable expertise and knowledge** to organizations, providing a foundation for future improvements. A **systematic approach** to change management fosters employee confidence and empowers them to embrace new initiatives.

Following a **proven method,** such as **setting clear goals, effective communication and training,** and involving employees in the change process, builds confidence in adapting and succeeding. Employees become more comfortable with change, knowing there is a structured approach to guide them.

⇒ If a customer service improvement initiative successfully reduces complaint resolution time, the organization can leverage this success to enhance customer satisfaction and explore improvements in other areas of the customer experience.

⇒ If a company implements a new software system successfully, employees gain confidence in adapting to technological advancements, making them more open to future changes and embracing opportunities for growth and innovation.

Empowering Employees:

Empowered employees become **influential change agents** within the organization, driving continuous improvement. They develop leadership skills, gain confidence, and inspire others to embrace change.

⇒ A manufacturing company established a cross-functional team to drive continuous improvement initiatives. This team, comprising employees from different departments and levels, represented diverse perspectives and areas of expertise. Given the authority to identify opportunities, propose solutions, and implement changes, this empowerment fostered ownership and collaboration. The result was a culture where continuous improvement was embraced and celebrated throughout the organization.

Promoting Innovation:

Organizations that prioritize continuous improvement also prioritize innovation. They create an environment that fosters and rewards innovation, encouraging employees to **think creatively, challenge the status quo**, and propose new ideas for improvement. Idea generation channels, such as suggestion programs or cross-functional brainstorming sessions, are established to capture and nurture innovative thinking.

⇒ ABC Tech encourages employees to submit innovative ideas through their innovation portal. Successful ideas are awarded resources and support, resulting in breakthrough innovations and process improvements.

Role of Change Agents:

Change agents play a crucial role in driving continuous improvement and growth. They serve as catalysts for change, **leading the way and inspiring others** to embrace new ideas and practices. Engaging in change initiatives enhances employees' leadership skills, enabling them to effectively collaborate and drive progress.

Leveraging Feedback and Continuous Learning:

Organizations that prioritize feedback and continuous learning create a culture of **adaptation, innovation, and improvement**. They establish feedback mechanisms and document lessons learned to facilitate ongoing learning and enhancement.

⇒ A business implements regular surveys to gather feedback from customers on their experience with a new product. The feedback received helps identify areas where improvements can be made, such as product features, customer support, or delivery processes. This feedback enables the organization to make iterative improvements and provide a better customer experience.

Setting New Goals and Objectives:

As organizations grow and evolve, ensure that new goals and objectives align with the overall strategic direction. This ensures that the continuous improvement efforts contribute to the organization's long-term success.

⇒ If a company's strategic direction is to expand into new markets, the goals and objectives for continuous improvement may include increasing market share in specific target regions or developing new product lines to meet the needs of those markets.

"In a culture of continuous improvement, learning, empowerment, and innovation flourish, fostering ongoing success and positioning organizations for sustainable growth in a rapidly evolving business landscape."

Improve & grow

- Foster a culture of continuous improvement and innovation.

- Encourage sharing ideas and suggestions for improvement.

- Promote a culture of innovation and agility

- Develop strategies for ongoing support, updates, and improvements.

- Celebrate achievements.

- Implement changes and enhancements based on feedback, data analysis, and lessons learned.

- Continuously optimize processes, systems, and strategies.

- Embrace a mindset of relentless learning and adaptation.

- Reward efficiency, accuracy, and growth.

- Reflect on lessons learned and apply them for future endeavors.

Going Paperless: Electronic Batch Record Project

In the culmination of the Electronic Batch Record (EBR) project, we successfully implemented a new technology that revolutionized the manufacturing processes. This complex project, encompassing significant changes in people, processes, and infrastructure, proved to be a resounding success, delivering the intended benefits within the scheduled timeframe.

Throughout **Step 5: Improve & Grow**, we focused on the closure of the project and the long-term benefits to our organization. We conducted a comprehensive lesson learned exercise, capturing valuable insights and experiences from the implementation. This exercise allowed us to reflect on the challenges we faced, the strategies we employed, and the key learnings that guided future endeavors.

In addition, we diligently documented our methodology and tools, ensuring that the knowledge gained from this project was preserved for future reference. These resources served as a valuable reference point, enabling the team to replicate our success in similar projects and further enhance our processes.

Despite the complexity of the EBR project, our team was fully engaged and committed to its success. Throughout the journey, their competencies and leadership skills were elevated to a new level. They demonstrated exceptional dedication, collaboration, and innovation, ensuring that the project was executed with utmost efficiency and effectiveness.

The benefits derived from the EBR implementation far exceeded our expectations. We achieved improved accuracy, traceability, and accessibility of data in our manufacturing processes. Efficiency and productivity were greatly enhanced, enabling us to optimize resource allocation and meet customer demands more effectively. Furthermore, the successful implementation of this technology reinforced the strategic plan to extend its application to other manufacturing areas, amplifying its impact throughout the organization.

As the EBR project concluded, I transitioned to new responsibilities, confident in the capable hands of our team. They took on the challenge of implementing these changes in other areas of the organization, leveraging the lessons learned and their newfound expertise. This exemplified our commitment to change, leadership and growth, as we continued to embrace future opportunities and drive continuous improvement throughout the organization.

The success of the EBR project served as a testament to our methodology, the dedication of our team, and the transformative power of effective change management. It reinforced our belief that by empowering our employees, nurturing a culture of continuous improvement, and leveraging innovative technologies, we could drive positive change and achieve remarkable results.

Change led us, and in turn, we led change. As we celebrated

the accomplishments of the EBR project, new opportunities arrived. The organization navigated new challenges, seized opportunities, and continued to grow resilient and agile.

This is how we embraced change, led transformation and fostered growth.

What's Next?

Congratulations on completing this journey of implementing changes! Armed with the knowledge and strategies outlined in this book, you are now equipped to be the catalyst of transformation in your organization. The power to drive change and shape the future lies within you.

Remember, change is not something to fear or avoid. It is an opportunity for growth, innovation, and ultimately, success. By embracing change and leading others through it, you have the chance to make a lasting impact on your organization and its people.

Now is the time to take action and be the champion of change. Inspire those around you with your enthusiasm and vision. Share the successes and lessons learned from this change initiative and let them serve as steppingstones for future endeavors.

Continue to foster a culture that thrives on change. Encourage open communication, collaboration, and learning. Embrace continuous improvement as a way of life, always seeking new ways to enhance processes and exceed expectations.

Remember, change begins with you. Lead by example and motivate others to join you on this exciting journey. Share stories of triumph and resilience and highlight the positive outcomes that arise from embracing change.

Share your stories with us at **info@MLGrowth.com**. We are excited to hear about your journey of change!

As you move forward, seize every opportunity to make a difference. Embrace new technologies, explore emerging trends, and challenge the status quo. Together, we can create a future where change is not only expected but celebrated as the driving force behind progress.

So, go forth and be the change agent your organization needs. Embrace change as an opportunity for growth and innovation. Your actions today will shape the future and inspire others to embark on their own change journeys.

Remember, you have the power to make a difference. Embrace change, take action, and watch your organization thrive in a world where adaptability and resilience are the keys to success.

The time for change is now. Are you ready to take the lead?

Change, Lead and Grow!

"Embrace change, navigate growth,
and unlock your limitless potential.
Together, we can create a world
of positive transformation."

Section II

Tool Kit

To have ongoing success, it is essential to establish systems in your business that align with your needs and the nature of your operations. In this section, you will find a list of tools that can be utilized based on the complexity, type and specific requirements of your business.

This is a list that will help you start and guide you in this process. As you progress through each step, the information gathered in each form or template will be used as building blocks to complete key actions in the subsequent stages.

This is process is not overly complicated. By dedicating time and preparing your team to effectively implement these changes, you will pave the way for ongoing success. Your journey will be a transformative experience for both your business and your employees.

Templates

- **Change Scope Overview**
- **Stakeholders List**
- **Impact Assessment**
- **Stakeholder Analysis**
- **Communication Plan**
- **Training Needs Assessment**
- **Training, Coaching, Development Plan**

- **Action Plan**

- **Risk Mitigation Plan**

- **Status Update Report**

- **Survey**

Templates serve as guidelines and can be customized to align with the specific needs and characteristics of your organization and change initiative.

Change Scope Overview

Include the following change information below.

Title: _____

Current State: _____

Future State: _____

What is the Change? _____

Why is it needed? _____

What are the drivers of the Change?

External: _____

Internal: _____

How does it align with the vision? _____

Benefits: _____

Risks: _____

Expected Results: _____

Location(s): _____

Functional Area(s): _____

Business Process(es): _____

Timing: _____

Templates serve as guidelines and can be customized to align with the specific needs and characteristics of your organization and change initiative.

Stakeholders List

Identify each Stakeholder (Group or Individual) and provide the information below.

Stakeholder Name - _____

Role - _____

Stakeholder Classification - _____

Interests - _____

Contact Information - _____

This information will be the used for the **Stakeholder Analysis.**

Templates serve as guidelines and can be customized to align with the specific needs and characteristics of your organization and change initiative.

Change Impact Assessment

Identify each Change Impact and provide the information below.

Area/Department - _____

Business Process - _____

Description of the Change - _____

Roles - _____

Type of Change Impact - (High/Medium/Low)

- People - _____

- Process - _____

- System - _____

Location - _____

Number of People Impacted - _____

Timing - _____

Benefits - _____

Risks - _____

Templates serve as guidelines and can be customized to align with the specific needs and characteristics of your organization and change initiative.

Stakeholder Analysis

Identify each Stakeholder (Group or Individual) and provide the information below.

Stakeholder Name - _____

Role(s) - _____

Stakeholder Classification - _____

Interest (WIIFM) - _____

Level of Impact - _____

Level of Influence - _____

Desired Level of Support - _____

Current Level of Support - _____

Contact Information - _____

Templates serve as guidelines and can be customized to align with the specific needs and characteristics of your organization and change initiative.

Communication Plan

Identify each Communication Channel and provide the information below.

Channel - _____

Objectives - _____

Key Messages - _____

Audience - _____

Owner - _____

Timing - _____

Reference Materials - _____

Templates serve as guidelines and can be customized to align with the specific needs and characteristics of your organization and change initiative.

Training Assessment

Identify each Change and Training Needs for each Stakeholder Group and provide the information below.

Change - _____

Gap Analysis - _____

Training Needs - _____

Stakeholder Group - _____

Size of Group - _____

Training and Development Methods - _____

Evaluation Plan - _____

Templates serve as guidelines and can be customized to align with the specific needs and characteristics of your organization and change initiative.

Training, Coaching and Development Plan

Identify each Training related information and provide the information below.

Training Identification - _____

Topics to be Covered - _____

Stakeholder Group - _____

Method of Delivery - _____

Materials to be Used - _____

Trainers and Coaches - _____

Schedule of Sessions - _____

Templates serve as guidelines and can be customized to align with the specific needs and characteristics of your organization and change initiative.

Action Plan

Identify each action plan and provide the information below:

Action Item	Responsible	References	Start Date	End Date	Status

Templates serve as guidelines and can be customized to align with the specific needs and characteristics of your organization and change initiative.

Risk Mitigation Plan

Identify each risk and provide the information below:

Risk Identification	Mitigation Strategy	Owner

Templates serve as guidelines and can be customized to align with the specific needs and characteristics of your organization and change initiative.

Survey

Instructions: Please rate your readiness for the upcoming change initiative on a scale of 1 to 5, with 1 being the lowest and 5 being the highest. This assessment will help gauge your preparedness and identify areas that may require additional attention and support. Consider the following questions:

Awareness and Understanding:

a. I am aware of the upcoming change and its objectives.

b. I understand the reasons behind the change and its importance to the organization.

c. I have a clear understanding of how the change aligns with the organization's goals and vision.

d. I understand the potential benefits and impact the change will have on the organization.

WIIFM (What's In It For Me):

a. I understand how the change will personally benefit me and my work.
b. I can identify how the change will positively impact my role and responsibilities.
c. I see the value of embracing the change and believe it will enhance my professional growth.

Role Clarity and Confidence:

a. I understand my role and responsibilities in the change initiative.
b. I am confident in my ability to fulfill my role effectively during the change process.
c. I have the necessary resources, tools, and support to perform my role in the change initiative.

Communications and Information:

a. I have received clear and consistent communications regarding the change initiative.
b. I am aware of the communication channels available to obtain relevant information about the change.
c. I feel informed about the progress and updates related to the change initiative.

Training and Development:

a. I have received the necessary training to develop the skills and knowledge required for the change.

b. I feel confident in my ability to apply the newly acquired skills in my work.

c. I have access to ongoing training and support to enhance my capabilities during the change process.

Change Acceptance and Adaptability:

a. I am open to embracing the change and its potential positive outcomes.

b. I am willing to adapt my work practices to align with the change initiative.

c. I believe that the change will contribute to the overall success of the organization.

Thank you for participating in this readiness assessment. Your responses will help us understand your level of preparedness for the upcoming change and identify any areas that may require additional support. We will use this information to tailor our communication, training, and support efforts to ensure a smooth transition and successful adoption of the change initiative.

Templates serve as guidelines and can be customized to align with the specific needs and characteristics of your organization and change initiative.

One Last Message!

In this book, you have learned about the five (5) steps to achieve ongoing success. Regardless of the size and complexity of your change, applying this framework will empower you to effectively manage change, lead your team through it, and foster the growth of your business.

By embracing the right mindset, attitude, and taking purposeful actions, change becomes an opportunity for your personal and professional development. With *"Change, Lead and Grow"* as your guide, you will be equipped to reach new heights in your business, whether you are streamlining processes, navigating transitions, or pursuing expansion.

Thank you for embarking on this transformative journey with us. We are excited to support you in achieving your business goals and witnessing the positive impact of change. Together, let's take your business to the next level!

"Change is constant. Embrace it and grow!"

Acknowledgments

Throughout my journey, I have been fortunate to cross paths with numerous individuals who have shared their wisdom, experiences, and guidance, each leaving a good mark on my life. While it is impossible to mention each name, I extend my heartfelt appreciation to all of you who have played a role in shaping the insights shared in this book. Your contributions have been instrumental, and I am truly grateful for your presence in my life.

A special acknowledgment goes to our clients, partners, organizations and associations, whose invaluable collaboration and partnership have provided real-world experiences that have enriched my understanding of the challenges and opportunities inherent in managing changes and business growth. Your insights and feedback have been instrumental in shaping the practical aspects of the strategies presented in this book.

To the professors and educators who ignited my passion for knowledge during my school and university years, and to the supervisors, managers, and colleagues from various workplaces whose collaboration and mentorship have contributed profoundly to my understanding of change, management, leadership, and organizational dynamics, thank you.

To the mentors, coaches, trainers, and authors whose programs, training sessions, seminars, and books have broadened my horizons and deepened my insights, I extend my gratitude. Your guidance has been instrumental in shaping my perspective and approach.

A sincere thank you to the teams I have had the privilege to work with throughout the years. Your support and dedication have been the driving force behind the successful implementation of various projects, and I value the collective efforts we have put forth.

To my cherished family, friends, colleagues, and mentors, your encouragement and belief in my journey have been a constant source of strength. Your presence has made this journey meaningful, and I am deeply grateful for your support:

Luis Mustafa, Kevin Cook, Ren Tangonan, Doris González, Marian Díaz, Doris Miranda, José González, Alba Ambert, Vanessa Arroyo, Francisco García, José Deliz, Mike Harman, Annie Mariel Arroyo, Kevin Costello, Shardendu Goswami, Tony Pesante, Israel Bravo, Alberto Cordero, Teresita Rodríguez, Migdoel Rodríguez, Merbil González, Cuauhtémoc Godoy, Nydia Ugarte, Irbis Lugo, María A. Pérez, Berta Jiménez, Noel Dávila, Orlando Santiago, Jennifer Biaggi,

Amaury Maldonado, Andrés Vázquez, Rosa Colón, Antonio Otaño, Jaime Garay-Lehmann, José Román, Julio Morant, Marlyn Battle, Jeff Schaaf, Anita Paniagua, Braulio Mejía, Marilyn Guzmán, Migdoel Rodríguez, Héctor Goveo, Weston Lyon.

Tony Robbins, Jack Canfield, Marci Shimoff, Kevin Eastman, James Malinchak, John P. Kotter, John C. Maxwell, Nick & Megan Unsworth, Dean Graziosi, Lisa Liebermann-Wang, Kevin Harrington, Francine Cousineau, John Formica, Kane & Alessia Minkus, Jill Lublin, Idith Suarez, Ricardo Soto, Minerva Pérez, Yaritza Velázquez, Brenda Ruiz, Victor González (RIP), Nelson Cora, Ferdinand Rodríguez, Alexis Normandía, Lourdes Rodríguez, Exor Vargas, Anthony González, Jan McNeill, Jessica Salazar, Rosa Cancel, Vidalina & Carlos Echevarría.

While I may not be able to cite everyone on the list, please know that your impact has been significant, and I hold your contributions close to my heart.

About María de Lourdes

María de Lourdes, with 25+ years of experience, held management roles in pharmaceutical companies before establishing her own business in 2009. She is a Professional Industrial Engineer and has an MBA in Human Resources and Industrial Management degree with extensive international experience in manufacturing, supply chain, consumer, medical devices, and other areas and industries.

She is a Certified Project Management Professional, with advanced skills in leadership, team building, and personal development. She leads teams, evaluates business needs, and delivers integrated solutions from multiple perspectives.

Employing a strategic approach, María de Lourdes empowers companies to overcome challenges and achieve successful outcomes.

www.MLGrowth.com

Additional Resources
Bibliography &
Recommended Resources

Jeffrey M. Hiatt, Timothy J. Creasey (2012). *Change Management: The People Side of Change.* Prosci Learning Center Publications.

John P. Kotter (2012). *Leading Change.* Harvard Business Review Press

Jeffrey M. Hiatt (2006). *ADKAR: A Model for Change in Business, Government and our Community.* Prosci Learning Center Publications.

Project Management Institute
www.pmi.org

Institute of Industrial and Systems Engineers
www.iise.org

Change Lead and Grow Program

Our framework helps you overcome challenges by focusing on the right strategies, giving you actionable insight on how to grow fast.

www.MLGrowth.com/Change-Lead-Grow

Schedule a Call:

https://www.MLGrowth.com/schedule-a-call

Made in the USA
Middletown, DE
15 October 2023

40849707R00119